Cathedrals of Britain

Cathedrals of Britain

West, South West and Wales

Bernadette Fallon

First published in Great Britain in 2018 by
Pen & Sword History
an imprint of
Pen & Sword Books Ltd
47 Church Street
Barnsley
South Yorkshire
S70 2AS

ISBN 978 1 52670 396 5

Typeset in Ehrhardt by
Aura Technology and Software Services, India
Printed and bound in the UK by CPI Group (UK) Ltd,
Croydon, CR0 4YY

Pen & Sword Books Ltd incorporates the imprints of Pen & Sword
Archaeology, Atlas, Aviation, Battleground, Discovery, Family
History, History, Maritime, Military, Naval, Politics, Railways,
Select, Transport, True Crime, Fiction, Frontline Books, Leo
Cooper, Praetorian Press, Seaforth Publishing and Wharncliffe.

For a complete list of Pen & Sword titles please contact
PEN & SWORD BOOKS LIMITED
47 Church Street, Barnsley, South Yorkshire, S70 2AS, England
E-mail: enquiries@pen-and-sword.co.uk
Website: www.pen-and-sword.co.uk

Contents

Acknowledgements

Thanks to everyone who gave so generously of their time and expertise to help with the writing of this book:

Jo Bartholomew, Sarah Williams, Simon Barwood and Phillip Holroyd-Smith at Winchester Cathedral; Ellen Simpson at Winchester City Council; Clare Dixon and Christina Reid, Winchester Tourist Guides; Marie Thomas, Tricia Glass and Emily Naish at Salisbury Cathedral; Florence Wallace and Emma Kirkup at Visit Wiltshire; Ruth Clacee-Rowe and Lindsay Mann at Wells Cathedral; Rebecca Clifford-Jones and John Tuner at Visit Somerset; Andrew Webb at City of Wells; Rebecca Faull, Lorna Giles and Stuart McIntyre at Gloucester Cathedral; Ben Hau at Marketing Gloucester; Chris Bodkin, Diane Walker and John Campbell at Exeter Cathedral; Victoria Hatfield, Deborah Lewis and Claire Toze at Visit Exeter; Catherine Marks at St Davids Cathedral; Pamela Thompson and Linda Mathias at St Asaph's Cathedral; Jane Harris, Sian Creak and Emma Warburton at Visit Wales; Evelina Andrews and Rebecca Lowe at Visit England.

Introduction

Spaces filled with centuries of human aspiration after the divine; in them, spiritual yearning is made palpable through stone.

Martin Barnes, *The English Cathedral*

The west of England and Wales is an area rich in countryside and traditional landscapes, scenic coasts and pretty towns. And also in cathedrals. Here you'll find many superlatives, many unique statistics. From Britain's longest cathedral, at Winchester, to its smallest, at St Asaph. From the tallest spire in the country – Salisbury – to the longest Gothic stone vaulted ceiling in the world – Exeter.

Here you'll find the cathedral founded in the country's smallest city, St Davids, by the man who would become the patron saint of Wales. In Gloucester, you'll find one of only six abbeys saved from destruction during the purge of the Reformation. And in Wells, one of the most impressive and famous cathedral fronts in the country, decorated with one of the largest collections of medieval statues in Europe.

The number of people visiting cathedrals in Britain has generally been rising since the start of the new millennium and several cathedrals are listed in the UK's top twenty most visited attractions every year. Attendance at cathedral worship is also rising, particularly at mid-week services. It's difficult to pinpoint exactly why this is happening now. These buildings have been impressive and unique for a very long time.

Winchester Cathedral is one of the biggest medieval churches in the world, founded in the city that was the original capital of England when the country was first united in the 10th century. The holy site of Wells has been attracting pilgrims for almost 2,000 years and has had a cathedral for nearly 1,000. Salisbury Cathedral was completed in only thirty-eight years and also holds the record for the highest spire in England, a record it has held for 700 years.

Gloucester Cathedral is a rarity, a true – and very lucky – survivor. This former abbey was only one of six to be spared when King Henry VIII's soldiers went through the country ransacking religious houses. Exeter Cathedral is said to have once held part of the true cross of Jesus Christ.

St Asaph's in Wales has intriguing links to Scotland and the founding saint of one of its most important cites. St Davids Cathedral has links across Europe and as far as Jerusalem. And this community, in what is today Britain's smallest city, was converted to Christianity long before St Augustine, the man credited with bringing Christianity to England in 597, landed on Britain's shores.

David was born in Pembrokeshire in Wales around 500AD and today the site of his birth is said to be marked by the ruins of a small ancient chapel, close to a holy well, on the cliffs at what is today called St Non's Bay. Non was David's mother. St Patrick, the patron saint of Ireland, who travelled from Britain to convert the Irish to Christianity in the 5th century, is also said to have connections with this part of Wales. Some say he came from this area. But whatever about Patrick, it's clear that David was spreading the word of God in Wales and beyond quite a while before Augustine arrived in 597.

Being early converts to the Christian faith didn't mean a thing when it came to the 16th-century Reformation, however. When he decided to split from the Catholic church in Rome – and grant himself a divorce from his wife in the process – King Henry VIII made no distinction between the English and Welsh churches, monasteries and abbeys. All were ransacked and plundered. The Catholic Church was abandoned and the Church of England and Wales established. The Act of Supremacy passed in 1534 stated that 'the king, our sovereign lord, and his heirs and successors, shall be taken, accepted and reputed as the only supreme head on earth of the Church of England'. And so the pope was abolished.

This state of affairs continued until 1920, when the church in Wales was separated from the Church of England and became an independent part of the Anglican community. Today it has its own elected archbishop and bishops and its own bilingual liturgy and calendar, as well as a governing body that is the equivalent of the Church of England's General Synod. It's a reversion to the old ancient order laid down by David, who was the first Archbishop of Wales.

The old ancient order itself harks back to the tradition of worship laid down in prehistoric times. Beside the 13th-century ruins of St Non's Chapel, standing stones in a nearby field suggest the chapel was built close to an ancient Pagan stone circle. Today the area is still an important place of pilgrimage and St Non's Retreat Centre offers a variety of retreats, workshops and events.

Across the country, churches and monasteries were placed close to the sites of sacred springs, megalithic monuments and Pagan shrines. The medieval pilgrim routes follow the same paths as prehistoric trails to holy wells and ritual spaces in the same way as our modern roads follow the line of ancient paths.

And it continues. The holy island of Lindisfarne was home to the Irish monk Aidan who founded a monastic cathedral on the island and travelled from there throughout the country, spreading Christianity across Britain. Today the island is still a place of pilgrimage, with several retreat houses offering organised events, as well as personal reflection time, carrying on a tradition that was established in the 7th century.

The west of the country is home to ancient monuments of immense significance to the people who created them, a link that is continued by our 'modern' monuments, the cathedrals of the Middle Ages. From Stonehenge, close to Salisbury, built with stones that most likely came from Wales, to nearby Silbury Hill and the stone circle at Avebury, and Glastonbury Tor, near the city of Wells, these mighty memorials were built to commemorate and remember, to leave a record for future generations, in the way our cathedrals do today.

Writing in the introduction to Peter Marlow's wonderful photographic record of forty-two English Anglican cathedrals, *The English Cathedral*, curator Martin Barnes calls these mighty buildings: 'Spaces filled with centuries of human aspiration after the divine; in them, spiritual yearning is made palpable through stone.'

Talking of his project, to photograph the nave of each of the cathedrals in the early morning light as the sun came up, Marlow himself said: 'How many times a year do you wake up excited by what is going to happen that day? I felt that way on most of my cathedral days.'

And, as I got up in the morning on my own 'cathedral days', travelling around the country to visit each of the beautiful buildings featured in the four books of the *Cathedrals of Britain* series, I felt it too. Excited to find out more about the stories that have shaped each of these buildings and created the legacy they pass on to future generations. Today they're still shaping, still creating. And so, the story continues.

Chapter 1

Winchester

Power, glory and dead Saxon kings

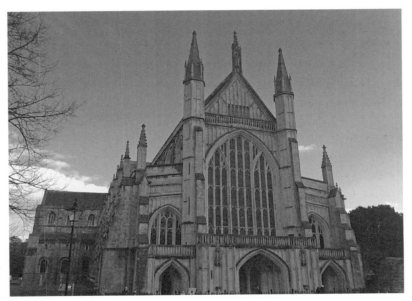

Winchester Cathedral. (© *Bernadette Fallon*)

Winchester Cathedral is vast. It is the longest cathedral in Britain, stretching 169m from the west entrance to the east end, and one of the biggest medieval churches in the world. Its stone floor is cracked and uneven, worn by centuries of pilgrims, and part of it even slopes gently downhill in places. But whatever its physical state, its spiritual place is among the elite.

The cathedral is in the one-time capital city of England and is one of the country's most important. Winchester was established as England's capital by the Saxon King Alfred, centuries before London laid claim to the title.

Winchester nave. (© *Bernadette Fallon*)

Building began on the cathedral in 1079 by William the Conqueror seven years after his victory at Hastings. It was consecrated in 1093, a mere twenty years later. Stones from the old minster, the former church that had occupied part of the site, were used in its construction, creating a link between the old and established and the new and Norman. There were other links too, including its important patron saint, as we shall see.

The original church was built on the orders of King Cenwalh around 648 in the traditional shape of a cross. And while William's eventual replacement followed the cruciform layout, the new structure dwarfed its predecessor. The cathedral's new nave alone was longer than the whole of the former Saxon church.

Today the nave is a reworking of that original Romanesque style into the Perpendicular Gothic of the late 14th century, when the three-storey nave was completely remodelled into the current two-storey structure. Pointed arches stretch to the heavens and the vault soars majestically above, its exquisite detailing all achieved with stone.

However, you'll still find parts of the original Romanesque building in the transepts. The Norman three-tier structure, with its lower-level arched arcade; the triforium in the middle; and the narrow windows of the clerestory at the top. Stand outside to get a true sense of the combination of architectural styles, the rounded Romanesque windows becoming pointed Gothic arches along the length of the building.

In fact, all of the major architectural periods are represented in Winchester Cathedral, from the early Anglo-Norman crypt to the Late Gothic of the presbytery aisles. And as well as linking different architectural styles through the ages, the building also carries reminders of its Saxon past and Winchester's royal connection as the seat of kings. Mortuary chests around the walls of the presbytery, close to the high altar, contain the bones of Saxon kings and their successors, including the 7th-century King

Cynegils, Egbert, the first king of the English, Ethelwulf, the father of King Alfred the Great, Canute, King of England, Denmark and Norway, and the early bishops of Winchester. The bones came from the original Saxon cathedral and were moved to the new building in the early 1100s, though not in any great order. Bones were jumbled together in the crypt under the presbytery and later brought up above ground in the early 1500s. The parliamentarians threw all the bones away during a raid on the cathedral during the Civil War, but many were rescued and returned to the mortuary boxes. By then it was anyone's guess which bones were which.

Curious facts: the saint who made it rain

The other famous link between past and present is the cathedral's original patron saint who was enshrined in the heart of the new cathedral. Once the Normans had finished their magnificent building, they reverently placed the silver chest containing the bones of the Saxon St Swithun in the greatest place of honour, the high altar.

Swithun was Bishop of Winchester from 852 to 863, advisor to King Alfred's father Aethelwulf, and most likely a tutor to the young King Alfred himself. He performed many miracles during his life – including restoring a broken set of eggs back to their unbroken state – and the miracles continued after his death. Following his wishes, he was buried outside the west door of Winchester's Saxon cathedral but was later moved inside so pilgrims could visit his relics in a decorated silver chest.

Swithun didn't like it. Legend has it that it rained for forty days and nights after the move because of the saint's displeasure. Which gave rise to the popular story that if it rains on St Swithun's Day, 15 July, it will continue to rain for forty days after. And this – if you are familiar with English weather – is sometimes quite likely:

St Swithun's day if thou dost rain
For forty days it will remain
St Swithun's day if thou be fair
For forty days 'twill rain nae mare

St Swithun's memorial. (© *Bernadette Fallon*)

The high altar in the new cathedral might be a sufficiently reverent place for the patron saint's relics, but it wasn't the most practical location for pilgrims to access. One of Winchester's early – and most important – bishops, Henry of Blois, had a solution. Inspired by a similar structure he had seen in St Peter's in Rome, he built a 3m tunnel through which pilgrims could crawl under the shrine to get close to the saint, lighting their way with a lit taper.

You can still see where Swithun's tunnel began in the east end of the cathedral. And a flight of steps from the north transept marks the pilgrims' way up to the shrine, leading to a striking 'carpet' of ceramic tiles, featuring over sixty different designs. These were laid in the 1200s and today are a mix of the 13th-century originals and reproductions. So now, not only are you following the same route as the early pilgrims, you are also stepping on some of the tiles they walked on. Overall, this is the largest surviving area of tiles from this period.

Today you don't need to crawl through a tunnel to pay your respects to Swithun. A metal frame with candle holders at each corner is a modern memorial to the saint and was made to mark the 1,100th anniversary of his death. Like so many other medieval saints of the time, his relics did not survive the destruction of the Reformation, when his shrine was demolished.

Demolished, but not completely lost, however. While the shrine was broken up, pieces of it were used as building materials elsewhere in the cathedral and, to date, over twenty pieces have been re-discovered.

Don't miss: the writer in the nave

One of the most famous and visited graves in the cathedral is in the nave. In May 1817, the author Jane Austen, suffering from illness, came to Winchester with her sister Cassandra to consult a doctor. They took lodgings near the cathedral on College Street. Her illness went undiagnosed and sadly Jane died here on 18 July. Though her illness was not even named in medical circles until the 1830s, judging by her symptoms it appears that she may have had Addison's Disease, a rare disorder of the adrenal glands.

Her tomb is marked by a stone in the floor of the nave, placed there by her brother Henry. Paying glowing tribute to the 'benevolence of her

Jane Austen memorial. (© *Bernadette Fallon*)

heart, the sweetness of her temper and the extraordinary endowments of her mind', there is no mention of her writing. Penning novels wasn't a seemly occupation for a woman in the early 19th century and Jane was not yet as famous as she would go on to become.

Fifty years later her nephew, James Edward Austen-Leigh, had a brass plaque erected on a nearby wall, which acknowledges her life as an author in its opening words, 'Known to many by her writings.' Fittingly, he paid for the memorial with the profits of his book *A Memoir of Jane Austen* published in 1869 and reprinted as a second edition, with some of her previously unseen writing, in 1871.

But it wasn't until 1900 that a more worthy tribute to Jane Austen the writer was installed, paid for by public subscription. Her stained-glass window by the esteemed Charles Kempe sits directly above her memorial plaque – though it does need a bit of interpretation. St Augustine is at the top, a play on her name – the abbreviated form of Augustine is Austin. Beneath is King David – who is linked to the psalms – and St John – who wrote the gospel – and the remaining figures are the sons of the Korah, who wrote some of the most beautiful psalms in the Bible. Jane herself makes an appearance in the Latin inscription that reads, translated, *'Remember in the Lord Jane Austen who died July 18th A.D. 1817'.*

This is not her original resting place, however. One hundred and twenty years after her burial, Winchester cathedral installed its first central heating system and Jane had to be moved six inches to the north to make way for the pipe running through the nave.

Who else is buried in the cathedral?

It's fitting that the two bishops buried in the nave were the two men who did so much to remodel it. Work here was started by Bishop Edington between 1346 and 1366. As well as a bishop, he was also treasurer to King Edward III, chancellor of England and the first prelate of the Order of the Garter, the medieval group of honourable knights set up by King Edward III, inspired by the tales of King Arthur and the knights of the round table. The bishop's alabaster effigy in his chantry chapel is one of the cathedral's finest medieval sculptures.

Bishop Edington's work was continued on a grand scale by his successor Bishop Wykeham, who completely remodelled the Norman nave into the soaring Gothic structure we see today. Wykeham lies in a magnificent chantry chapel, its location specially picked out by the bishop before his death. As a young boy, William heard mass said by his favourite monk, Richard Pekis, at an altar in the aisle. As Bishop of Winchester, he had his chantry chapel built on the spot where he had once stood and listened. Today it is cared for by Winchester College and New College Oxford, both of which he founded.

Don't miss: the chantry chapels

Throughout the cathedral many chantry chapels have survived and you'll find several of the most important in the retrochoir. The chapel of Bishop Stephen Gardiner is something of an anomaly, however, as chantries had in fact been forbidden by law by the time that Gardiner died in 1555.

He was an important man in the court of King Henry VIII, the king's loyal advisor and appointed Bishop of Winchester for his services, the last Roman Catholic to hold the role. But Henry's son, Edward VI, later had Gardiner imprisoned for refusing to enforce Protestant doctrine. He was released when the Catholic Queen Mary came to the throne, appointed Lord Chancellor and reinstated as Bishop of Winchester. In 1554, he conducted the marriage of Mary to Prince Philip of Spain in the cathedral.

William Waynflete, bishop from 1447 to 1486, was another very powerful and influential man, being also headmaster of Winchester College, Master and Provost at Eton, founder of Magdalen College Oxford, and Lord Chancellor of England. The intricate filigree carving around the outside of his chapel is particularly beautiful – look out for the snail carved in among the trailing roses.

And the royal roll-call continues. Cardinal Henry Beaufort, Bishop of Winchester from 1405 to 1447, was half-brother to King Henry IV, uncle to Henry V, great-uncle to Henry VI and three times Lord Chancellor of England. One of the richest men in the country, he left part of his fortune to the cathedral, which was used to build a new shrine for St Swithun and the wonderfully ornate great screen behind the high altar. It's thought he may have been involved in the trial of Joan of Arc, whose statue you will find nearby, outside the Lady Chapel, standing on a piece of stone from the prison in Rouen where she was held prisoner.

Look out also for the restored vaulted ceiling with its magnificent colouring in the chapel of Bishop Langton, who shouldn't be here at all. He was nominated in 1550 as Archbishop of Canterbury, the highest religious honour in the land, but died of the plague before he could take it up.

Outside the retrochoir in the south presbytery aisle you'll find Richard Fox, Henry VII's secretary of state, the founder of Corpus Christi College Oxford, and Bishop of Winchester from 1501 to 1528. It's one of the cathedral's two cadaver tombs, with the effigy depicted as a chillingly realistic decaying corpse designed to show the transient nature of life – even for a royal secretary of state.

In total, Winchester has seven chantries, built between the 14th and 16th centuries. Up to the reign of King Henry VIII, the Bishop of Winchester was the first English bishop in rank behind the archbishops of Canterbury and York, and Winchester was the wealthiest see in England, controlling one third of the country's riches.

Not all of the mighty chapels are dedicated to bishops, however. The Fishermen's Chapel is dedicated as a memorial to Izaak Walton, who was buried under the grey stone facing its entrance in 1683. His most famous book *The Compleat Angler* is a tribute to the pleasures of fishing and the beauty of nature, and the contemporary altar,

Bishop Fox's cadaver tomb. (© *Bernadette Fallon*)

carved in 1995, incorporates many of the fish mentioned in the book into its design. The stained-glass window features the fishermen-apostles Peter and Andrew, as well as Walton himself, who lived in the Cathedral Close for the last years of his life.

Don't miss: the man who saved the cathedral

There is one other memorial you shouldn't miss. While the bishops were fundamental in building and maintaining this great cathedral, the fact that it is still standing today is down to the

William Walker memorial. (© *Bernadette Fallon*)

work of a single man. He's not a member of the clergy though, but a dockyard diver.

You'll find William Walker in the east end of the retrochoir, a bronze sculpture carved in tribute to the man who saved Winchester Cathedral from sinking into the ground. Built on soft peat, its beech tree foundations started to rot after drainage work opened them up to the air. By the start of the 20th century, it was clear that urgent work needed to be done to save the cathedral from collapse. This work involved underpinning the foundations of the building to a level of 6m beneath the surface – and under water.

To carry out the job and make the building safe, the diver William Walker submerged himself in thick murky water in complete darkness, six hours a day, for six years. He dug out the peat, removed the rotting wood and laid bags of concrete to create a new solid base under the building.

After the job was done, he attended a service of thanksgiving for his work on St Swithun's Day 1912, which was also attended by King George V and Queen Mary. He was later made a Member of the Royal Victorian Order. He died, aged just 49, in the Spanish flu epidemic of 1918. Many years later his sculpture was unveiled, a monument to the man who had saved the cathedral with his bare hands.

Curious facts: they got the wrong man

Though what you see today is the second version of the sculpture, unveiled in 2001. It shows Walker dressed in his diving gear and holding his helmet, equipment that weighed over 90kg. It also shows his prominent moustache, for which he was famous. An earlier, clean-shaven model is thought to have been a representation of the engineer on the project, mistakenly picked out of a group photo as Walker by the original sculptor.

Don't miss: the artist in the crypt

With the water table so close to the ground surface, the crypt regularly floods, rendering the arresting lone figure there all the more poignant, standing up to his knees in water. The sculpture, Sound II, was a gift from the contemporary artist Antony Gormley, made from lead from a cast of his own body and created as an encouragement towards stillness. It's not the only water in the crypt. A well lies beneath the original position of the high altar, as was traditional in ancient cathedrals.

The crypt is the oldest part of the cathedral, built soon after 1079. Unusually, it was not designed to bury the dead but to raise the floor of the presbytery above, elevating the high altar to echo the 'holy hill' of Jerusalem and its temple.

Behind the altar sits the great screen, with the figure of Christ on the cross at its centre. It was completed by 1475 and, as we have learned, came from Bishop Beaufort's great bequest. Its statues date from the Victorian era, the originals not having survived the Reformation intact, though the remains of some of them are on display in the Triforium Gallery. And the striking altar tapestry provides a link into the 21st century. Created by artist Maggie Hambling, its wonderful abstract swirls depicting the strength and force of nature.

Beside the presbytery, the quire with its ornate 14th-century oak stalls showcases some of the finest medieval carving in England. The decorated canopies sprout foliage, animals, mythical creatures, human forms and several green men. Underneath, the misericord 'mercy seats' feature a fascinating mix of scenes and stories, including a veiled nun cavorting in the bushes, a cat carrying a mouse in its teeth and a squirrel nibbling a hazel nut. These seats have a ledge underneath, against which the clergy could rest during long hours of worship standing in the quire.

Winchester screen and altar tapestry. (© *Bernadette Fallon*)

Don't miss: the *Winchester Bible*

This famous bible is one of the cathedral's most treasured possessions, dates from the mid-12th century and was probably commissioned by Henry of Blois. As well as Bishop of Winchester from 1129 to 1171, he was also Abbot of Glastonbury Abbey, the grandson of William the Conqueror and brother of Stephen, King of England. There is also a good chance he may be buried in the 12th-century tomb in the cathedral quire.

The bible is exquisitely detailed with glowing colours, including gold and lapis lazuli from Afghanistan, which were among the most expensive and difficult to obtain in those times, showing no expense was spared on its creation. Neither were many calves. Two hundred and fifty were slaughtered to make the delicate vellum pages that carry the illuminated script.

And, surprisingly, it was written by a single monk, no mean feat in a book of nearly 1,000 pages. Which makes the occasional mistake a bit more understandable and you can still see some of the corrections that were made in the margins. A team of travelling craftsmen added the illuminated illustrations, six different artists have been identified by their varying styles. Of these, the artist dubbed 'The Master of the Leaping Figures' has produced some of the most exciting work – the clue is in his name. A true traveller, his work has been tracked as far as Spain.

The bible still exists today because it was never finished, so never used and thus preserved. It's had an eventful history, which has included spending time in London during the Civil War until Cromwell ordered its return to Winchester. Several of its pages 'disappeared' in the 19th century and were later offered to the artist William Morris for £170, but Morris declined to buy them. The pages were eventually bought by the banker J.P. Morgan for $6,000 and ended up in the Morgan Library in New York. Today the bible is used for important ceremonies in the cathedral, when it is carried in procession through the building.

William Morris might not have ended up with the pages of the *Winchester Bible*, but he does have a connection with Winchester Cathedral. Three of the windows in the epiphany chapel came from his workshop. They were designed by fellow artist Edward

Burne-Jones and tell the story of the birth of Jesus in the classic Pre-Raphaelite style.

You can see the work of another famous artist in the Lady Chapel, with its beautiful stained-glass by Charles Kempe showing Jesse, the founding father of ancient Israel, whose twelve sons each headed one of its tribes. Accordingly, it features a lot of men, but three women also make an appearance. These include the Virgin Mary – as it's her chapel – and Queen Victoria, depicted in honour of her Diamond Jubilee in 1897. The window was unveiled by the queen's daughter Princess Beatrice, who commended the artist on the wonderful likeness he had achieved of her mother. Mr Kempe later remarked to the dean that it was a wonder indeed, as he had used his cook as the model.

Victorian sensibilities were suitably offended on the installation of the memorial to the Portal family in the nave in 1897. French Huguenots, they fled to England to avoid Catholic persecution, set up a paper mill and made their fortune making paper for English banknotes at a time when the colonies were expanding and banknotes were in growing demand. But the angel at the centrepiece of the monument was deemed unsuitably clothed, with her belly button clearly protruding through her virtually see-through negligee. As are her breasts. And not only that, the sculptor apparently used his mistress as the model.

Back in the nave, stand at the font, which is the most famous of the black Tournai fonts in England and carved with stories from the life of St Nicholas. Look towards the great west window to see if you can make out the images in the stained-glass. You may have some difficulty. After the destruction of windows in the Civil War, fragments of glass from all around the building were randomly re-assembled here – legend has it by the people of Winchester themselves. Reportedly more than sixty percent of the glass is medieval, from the 14th century. Today it offers a very modern effect, a contemporary 'abstract', albeit from the 17th century via the Middle Ages.

Portal memorial. (© *Bernadette Fallon*)

Visiting Winchester Cathedral

There is a fee to visit the cathedral outside of service times and this includes a guided tour. For more information visit the website at Winchester-cathedral.org.uk.

Winchester: where to go and what to do

Outside the cathedral, the surroundings of Cathedral Close offer much of historical interest, as well as pleasant lawns to relax and enjoy the views. Here you can trace the early history of Winchester's clerical power. The Inner Close, in the north part of the lawns, was once the main cloister of St Swithun's Priory, with the monks' dormitory, chapter house and refectory nearby. A beautiful walled garden now stands on the site of the dormitory and is open to visitors. In the Outer Close you'll find the excavated site of the Saxon old minster.

The deanery in the close, with its vaulted porch and pointed arches, dates from the 13th century. This former home of medieval priors was substantially rebuilt in the 17th century, but the prior's hall still has its fine 15th-century timber roof. It's now the home of the deanery bookstall, selling second-hand books to support the work of the cathedral's choir.

At the edge of the close you can see what is left of one of the early palaces of William the Conqueror in a very unexpected place. Go downstairs to the menswear department in the Hambledon store and you'll see the ancient arched vaults of his palace's wine cellar, now housing racks of shirts and lines of shoes, one of the most historically interesting boutiques in the world.

William's fortified castle stood at the top of the hill, on what is today's High Street, and miraculously part of it still remains wholly intact. The great hall was the only part of the 11th-century Winchester Castle not to be destroyed by Oliver Cromwell's troops in the Civil War, and it is here that you will find King Arthur's round table. Sadly, it's not an original but it still has an interesting provenance.

King Arthur, the legendary British ruler, led the defence of Britain against Saxon forces in the late 5th and early 6th centuries, though historians still debate the fact of his existence. His famed round table, around which he and his knights sat, became the stuff of legends. By the close of the 12th century it had come to represent the chivalric order associated with the court of King Arthur, the Knights of the Round Table.

This symbolic re-creation in Winchester's Great Hall was made in the late 13th century possibly for the betrothal of one of Edward I's daughters. In the reign of King Henry VIII, the table was painted with the Tudor rose at its centre and the figure of King Arthur on his throne, surrounded by the names of his knights including the famous Sirs Galahad, Lancelot and Gawaine.

The 12th-century Wolvesey Castle at the city walls is now a ruin but was once the home of several bishops of Winchester throughout the Middle Ages. It was also here that Queen Mary and Prince Philip celebrated their wedding feast, after their marriage in the cathedral in 1554. Today the Bishop of Winchester lives in Wolvesey Palace next door.

If you've visited the grave of Jane Austen, you might want to see the last place she lived before she died. Number 8 College Street is a private house and not open to the public, but many people still make a pilgrimage to stand outside and take photos. Or you could travel 18 miles outside the city to visit one of her former homes, now Jane Austen's House Museum in Chawton village. It's here she wrote *Mansfield Park*, *Emma* and *Persuasion*, and revised *Pride and Prejudice*, *Sense and Sensibility* and *Northanger Abbey*.

Winchester is full of attractive period buildings, atmospheric winding streets and charming riverside walks. The Keats Walk through the water meadows takes in the landscape said to have inspired his poem *To Autumn*.

If you want to base yourself as close as possible to the cathedral, opt for the Mercure Winchester Wessex Hotel, right on the edge of the cathedral grounds. This contemporary, comfortable hotel offers the most amazing views of the building, particularly at night as the lights come on. And it's only a short hop across the lawns to an early morning service when you wake.

Winchester is easily reached from London and the south by train, and is very well placed to access the south coast.

Chapter 2

Salisbury

The cathedral in the meadows

Salisbury Cathedral. (*Photo by Jacques Eloff ©: reproduced by kind permission*)

It's one of the most quintessentially English cathedrals and its spire is the tallest in the country. Set in lush meadows by a river, Constable painted about 300 different versions of it over his lifetime. And it is unusual among its medieval counterparts in not evolving piecemeal, section by section, but was built as a single creation in the 13th century.

It's actually the third establishment to hold the name of Salisbury Cathedral, but the first one to occupy this site. The first cathedral was started in 1075 in Old Sarum, about two miles north of Salisbury, and completed in 1091. Not the luckiest of establishments, five days after it was consecrated in 1092, it was struck by lightning, caught fire and burned down. Undeterred, the then bishop, Osmund, had it rebuilt and it was later extended under his successor Bishop Roger, and again by Bishop Jocelin. Today the outline of its foundations can still be clearly seen at the top of Old Sarum Hill.

Salisbury was then a fortified town and the Old Sarum cathedral was located within the outer walls of the Norman castle. There were constant clashes between the clergy and the soldiers, not enough houses for the canons to live in and the hilltop's windy location meant the choir could hardly hear itself sing. The pope was petitioned for a new site and The Close, the location of today's cathedral, was laid out in 1197. The first foundation stones were laid in 1220 and the cathedral was finished a mere thirty-eight years later, in 1258.

The style of Salisbury throughout, from its starting point in the east to the end of the nave, is English Gothic and the cathedral showcases each of the three phases of this architectural style: Early English; Decorated; and Perpendicular. It was built on a massive scale, no doubt to compete with the greats of Canterbury, Winchester and Lincoln, which were already in place by then. And it mostly remains as it was built nearly 800 years ago, with just three additions to the main structure made since the 13th century – the tower with its spire, strengthening arches at the crossing and a small chantry chapel.

The bodies of the bishops

But even though Salisbury is a rarity among cathedrals – built on an empty site, with no previous building history – there is a strong connection between past and present. You'll find it in the

Lady Chapel, the oldest part of the cathedral, properly named the Chapel of Holy Trinity and All Saints, or Trinity Chapel.

In 1226, the year after Trinity Chapel was consecrated, the bodies of three bishops of Old Sarum were re-interred here, including Bishop Osmund, who was responsible for completing the very first Salisbury Cathedral in 1091. His coffin lid is displayed in the centre of the chapel. And there's another poignant memorial here that links the chapel to contemporary times. We'll learn more about it later.

Curious facts: the water in the transept

When the spire was added to the top of the tower in the early 1300s, 6,500 extra tonnes of weight were added to the structure of the cathedral. But the foundations of the building are only 4 feet deep, so what keeps Salisbury standing? What keeps it up is the 27 feet of compact ground and water under the foundations. And in fact, you can remove a stone from the floor in the transept and dip a stick in the water underneath.

Water also creates one of the newest – and most arresting – features in the nave. Entering into the dramatic light-filled interior, with soaring arches and immense vaulted ceiling, the eye is next drawn to the spectacular font centrepiece. The Living Water Font was designed by British water sculptor William Pye and installed in 2008, on the eve of Michaelmas Day, as part of the 750th anniversary celebrations of the original consecration of the cathedral in 1258.

Presiding at the service, the Archbishop of Canterbury, the leader of the Church of England, consecrated the font and his cross made in oil is still visible on all four sides of the green patinated bronze vessel. The font is designed to present the continuous movement of water and is carved with the words from the *Bible*: 'When you pass through the waters, I will be with you.'

Water can also bring its own issues of course, and careful watch is kept on the water levels. The last serious flooding inside the cathedral

Salisbury font. (*Photo by Ash Mills ©: reproduced by kind permission*)

was in 1915 and reached ankle height. But in the 1630s, the flooding was reportedly so bad that the clergy had to ride around inside on horseback.

Light pours into the nave on all sides from the high Gothic windows, which are filled with clear glass. But medieval cathedrals at the time were all richly adorned with stained-glass. So where did it go?

The answer is into a ditch somewhere. Remarkably, this did not happen during the Reformation when so many cathedrals had their treasures stolen or destroyed under the orders of Henry VIII, seeking to remove all signs of Catholic worship. But as Salisbury Cathedral didn't have a monastery or abbey attached, it largely escaped the attention and the ravages of the king's troops. Instead its stained-glass was not removed until the late 18th century. Ironically, it was the man trusted with the cathedral's restoration from 1789 to 1792 who destroyed it – the architect James Wyatt, known in Salisbury as Wyatt the Destroyer.

Why did he do it?

There were probably a number of reasons behind his thinking. The *Bible* was now printed in English and so, rather than listening to it being read, the congregation were reading it for themselves. Stained-glass made the interior quite dark, clear glass filled it with light. There was also probably an element of 'out with the old, make way for the new', that comes with the desire for progress.

In another act of what is considered to be complete desecration, he whitewashed the nave ceiling, covering all of its coloured medieval paintings. You will see fragments of paintings in the transepts and around the quire area, but these are Victorian additions.

Luckily Wyatt didn't get around to removing all of the windows. Two grisaille windows from the 13th century survived and can be seen at the west end of the nave aisles. And Sir George Gilbert Scott, in his subsequent 19th-century renovation, had new stained-glass windows made to bring some light-filled colour into the building. In the south quire aisle you'll find two beautiful windows designed by Edward Burne-Jones and made by William Morris.

Don't miss: the oldest clock in the country

There's a complicated-looking piece of machinery close to the back of the nave. This is, in fact, a clock and not just any clock, it's very likely the oldest working mechanical clock in existence. It dates from about 1386, is hand-made from iron and, as was usual for the period, has no face, being designed merely to strike the 'prayer hour'.

The clock was originally kept in the bell tower but, when this was also demolished by Wyatt as another one of his 'improvements', it was moved into the cathedral tower. Here it continued to strike the hour until 1884, when a new clock was installed. The original clock went missing for a while but was happily rediscovered in 1929 and was repaired and restored to use in 1956.

Curious facts: the mysterious death of an earl

The 3rd Earl of Salisbury, William Longespee, had the honour of being the first person to be buried in the cathedral and today you'll find his tomb in the nave. He was the illegitimate son of King Henry II who ruled England from 1154 to 1189, and the half-brother of kings Richard and John. Richard plotted against his father to take the throne and John, in turn, plotted against Richard to get his hands on it. Both were ruthless, remembered as tyrants and it seems their half-brother, the earl, may have been just as unpopular, despite his successes leading English raids against France in the 13th century.

Why?

William was an important man, a member of the royal family and present at the signing of *Magna Carta* – of which one of only four remaining copies is held by Salisbury Cathedral. His wife, Ela of Salisbury, was an heiress and countess and a very good catch. After William failed to return from one of his military expeditions, presumed lost in the storm that had shipwrecked his fleet, Ela was under pressure to marry again but declined all offers. In fact, William had been rescued and was in a monastery on a French island, eventually returning home to his wife. A banquet

Hertford tomb. (© *Salisbury Cathedral: reproduced by kind permission*)

was given at Salisbury Castle to celebrate his return, during which the earl suddenly and mysteriously died and was buried in the new cathedral.

But the mystery deepens.

When his tomb was opened in 1719, a dead rat was found in his skull. Upon examination, it was found to have died from arsenic poisoning, presumably from ingesting the arsenic in the last body it fed on, the body of the earl. Did a thwarted suitor, annoyed by the earl's unexpected return, hope to finally win the hand of Ela by making her a widow? Roger of Wendover, a monk and chronicler of the 13th century, accused Hubert de Burgh, the first Earl of Kent, of the poisoning. The truth will never be known. But the rat continues. His remarkably well-preserved corpse is now on display in a case at the Salisbury and South Wiltshire Museum.

Other connections with royalty include the tomb of Edward Seymour. Seymour, the first Earl of Hertford, was married to Lady Catherine Grey, the sister of Lady Jane Grey, who was Queen of England for just nine days. Due to the family's claim on the throne, the earl and his wife spent a substantial amount of their lives in the Tower of London – but still managed to produce two children from the marriage. Their elaborate tomb is one of the largest in the country outside of Westminster Abbey.

Don't miss: the Audley Chapel

The original plan of the cathedral contained thirteen chapels, but over the centuries their layout and use has changed and the infamous Wyatt had a part to play here too. He demolished two medieval chantry chapels at the east end, but luckily left the Audley Chapel, with its stunning fan vaulted ceiling. Built for Edmund Audley, who was bishop in the cathedral from 1502 to 1524, it is a beautiful

Audley Chapel. (*Photo by Ash Mills ©: reproduced by kind permission*)

example of the Perpendicular style and the ceiling still has some of its original medieval colouring.

It's remarkable the colour has lasted, but what is more remarkable is that the carved details of roses and pomegranates survived. The roses were the symbol of King Henry VIII and are linked here with the pomegranates, the symbol of his first wife Catherine of Aragon. Ironically, the pomegranates represent fertility but after Catherine failed to produce a son and heir for Henry, he divorced her to marry Anne Boleyn, cutting himself and the whole country free of the Catholic church in the process. Very few pomegranates endured the purge that followed, these Salisbury talismans are a rare survival.

As well as removing a few chapels, all of the medieval nave paintings and most of the stained-glass, Wyatt also took away the screen separating the nave from the quire. This, however, had some benefits because, although it's sad to lose another piece of medieval architecture, the view from end to end of the cathedral that the removal has opened up is simply stunning.

Curious facts: the bishops in the quire

Inside the quire you'll find some of the oldest carved choir stalls in the country. The rear stalls were a gift from King Henry III in 1236. The misericord carvings under the seats in the stall also date from the 13th century, but the canopies overhead, with their statues representing the bishops of Salisbury, are early 20th-century. You may notice that one bishop is not wearing his mitre on his head. Instead it's at his feet, which seems a mark of great disrespect. But why?

John Salcot – also known as John Capon – was Bishop of Salisbury from 1539 to 1557, during some of the country's most tumultuous and bloody years, first under King Henry VIII, then King Edward VI, and finally Queen Mary. Starting out as a Catholic, he turned Protestant under Edward, then back to Catholic again to appease Mary. He was responsible for sending many to their deaths for disobeying the

Mompesson tomb. (© *Salisbury Cathedral: reproduced by kind permission*)

monarch's rule – though the rules very much depended on who was in power. Those put to death included some of his own parishioners who were burned at the stake in Salisbury.

The names on the seats in the quire are the names of the prebends, the original group of canons who founded the cathedral and donated part of their 'prebend' or income, to pay for its building. In return, they received land in the Cathedral Close where they built their houses. Some of the houses remain and a few are open to the public, including Arundells, the house where former prime minister Edward Heath lived until 2005. He is buried in the cathedral and you'll find the simple stone plaque that marks his grave in the floor close to the quire.

However, simple isn't a word you could apply to the tomb of Sir Richard Mompesson and his wife Kathleen. Sir Richard came from a family of minor gentry but married well and earned himself a place in the service of King James in 1603, for which he received a knighthood. He retired to a house in Salisbury, which was later rebuilt by a successor, Charles Mompesson, in 1701. It is now one of the main attractions in the close outside, as well as the setting for part of the film *Sense and Sensibility*. Sir Richard asked to be buried in the cathedral and the ornately decorated and brightly painted effigies of him and his wife lie in great state in the aisle. Except they are facing the wrong way. Moved from their original position to make place for the organ, they were subsequently accidentally placed facing west instead of east.

Don't miss: the 'banging' stone

Salisbury was the first cathedral in the country to recruit girl choristers, which it did in 1991. The girls' choir sings independently of the boys' choir in cathedral services and each consists of twenty choristers. The girls are initiated into the choir by being struck on the head three times with a bible. It might not sound pleasant but it's better than what the boys have to endure. They have their heads banged three times on a special 'banging stone' just outside the quire, which has a deep groove in the centre from centuries of little heads being struck against it.

Curious facts: the medieval cloisters

It's ironic that the cloisters at Salisbury Cathedral are the largest medieval cloisters in England. Built in 1266, strictly speaking they were not necessary at all, as cloisters are mainly connected with monasteries, providing space for monks to work and pray. But Salisbury never had a monastery.

These cloisters were designed for processions and today's processions pass under the same ceiling bosses that their 13th-century predecessors did. Out here some of the original coloured paint that would have decorated all of the cloisters – and the cathedral inside – is still visible.

Salisbury cloisters. (*Photo by Ash Mills ©: reproduced by kind permission*)

The chapter house is accessed through the cloisters and was also built in the 13th century. Its octagonal style is similar to that at Westminster Abbey and it features a beautiful fan-vaulted ceiling that rises from a central column. According to the author Daniel Defoe, who wrote an account of his travels through Wiltshire in the early 18th century, the column moved when he leaned against it. Though as it's still proudly standing 300 years later, it's difficult to know how accurate his impressions were.

The carved heads around the arches may represent the local community at the time of the building. Except for, hopefully, the three-headed individual above the bishop's seat, opposite the entrance. If you look closely you will see that the head on the left is facing a stone head that is sticking his tongue out in glee – right back at the bishop's chair.

Today the chapter house's most precious possession is the cathedral's copy of *Magna Carta*, one of only four surviving charters from 1215 and reportedly in the best condition. Comprising 3,500 words of Latin on sheepskin, making it much more expensive than the traditional calfskin commonly used in manuscripts, we know it was written by monks because of its decorative calligraphy. Over 800 years later, it still forms the basis of English law and individual liberty.

Salisbury Chapter house. (*Photo by Ash Mills ©: reproduced by kind permission*)

Above the east end of the cloister is the library, established by King Henry VI in 1445. He donated thirty oak trees to make the original bookcases and in return, his head was carved above the door to honour his generosity. Except that the growing collection made it eventually necessary to install another bookcase close by – and now his nose presses into it.

The library holds over 10,000 books in total, including a collection of sixty tomes that were made by the scribes at Old Sarum. The oldest holding dates from the 9th century, a page from the Old Testament written in Latin. There are 200 handwritten books here and early printed works include a second edition of Edmund Spenser's *The Faerie Queene* from 1611. An Oxford professor and founder member of the Royal Society, Seth Ward, who was Bishop of Salisbury from 1667 to 1689, donated a fascinating collection of early scientific and medical works.

Anyone in the market for organising a coronation will find the account of the coronation of James II in 1687 particularly interesting, including how-to details, full guest lists, seating plans and menus. The menus make fascinating reading and include neates' tongues,

Salisbury library. (© *Bernadette Fallon*)

tame pigeons, truffles, roasted udders and asparagus. There's also an intriguing copy of a 16th-century Latin textbook on the shelves – though readers should open with care. A handwritten note on the opening pages says 'the first mouse we caught this year was Aug 2', and is followed up on later pages with a piece of fur between the pages and – at the back of the book – a preserved and flattened medieval mouse.

Don't miss: the 'secret view'

High up on the gallery beneath the west window, you can enjoy a magnificent, uninterrupted view of the nave right through to the great east end. Here too you can see the 'behind the scenes' timber

Prisoner of Conscience window. (© *Salisbury Cathedral: reproduced by kind permission*)

beams that support the upper structures. These trees used in the building of the cathedral were growing in the 9th century, cut down after 200 years to lend support to a building that is 800 years old. Some of the wood is local, some is Irish, as King Henry III donated trees from his estates in Ireland and Wiltshire for the build.

Here too you can see up close the marks on the stones and timbers left by the masons and carpenters. Some are notes, some are communications and some are what appear to be drawings and symbols to ward off evil. Here are the concentric marks known colloquially as 'daisy wheels', designed to catch the devil, and also Marian marks, the double M sign, the symbol of the Virgin Mary.

Unfortunately, you'll have to gain access to a locked door at the end of the cathedral to get up there. However, the cathedral recently introduced a new graffiti tour to explain the fascinating medieval markings around the building. And this tour takes you up to the gallery.

We started the chapter in one of the very oldest parts of the cathedral, the Trinity Chapel. Today it tells one of its newest stories and is dedicated to the Prisoners of Conscience of Amnesty International. The Prisoners of Conscience Window in this chapel was installed in 1980 and includes faces of actual prisoners held in captivity for their beliefs. Every morning a prisoner is remembered here by name in the service.

From old to new, from medieval concerns to modern-day considerations, the cycle continues and the line of continuity remains unbroken at Salisbury.

Visiting Salisbury Cathedral

The cathedral asks visitors for a voluntary donation to help support and maintain the building, with a suggested contribution of £7.50 per adult. Guided tours within the cathedral are free and run regularly, tower tours may be booked for a fee. Library tours are also available to book, with the option of including a cream tea in the refectory. For more information visit Salisburycathedral.org.uk.

Salisbury: where to go and what to do

A quick look at a map of the city will show you how green it is, with its water meadows, parks and gardens, criss-crossed by the rivers Avon and Nadder. A punting trip down the river is a great way to get an alternative view of the cathedral, as well as a look at some local wildlife. Back in the city, the architecture is a mix of wonderfully atmospheric eras, from medieval walls to Tudor town houses and Georgian mansions to Victorian villas.

Start your explorations in Cathedral Close, a collection of beautiful buildings set in tranquil green gardens around the cathedral, many of which date back to the 13th century. Some you can peer at across walls covered in rambling foliage and some you can walk right into. One of these is Arundells, the former home of Edward Heath, prime minister of the United Kingdom from 1970 to 1974. Bequeathing the house to the nation after his death in 2005, it displays the former owner's eclectic collection of art, photographs, sailing paraphernalia and political memorabilia. Helpful guides in each room bring the collections to life and it's very enjoyable to wander at will through the beautiful rooms. The large garden at the back is a particular treasure, running right down to the river and affording atmospheric views of Salisbury's high spire.

The Salisbury Museum in the close provides a fascinating history of the area. Among the archaeological finds collected here is the Stonehenge Archer, the bones of a man found in a ditch surrounding the famous stone circle. The Wessex Gallery tells the ancient stories of Salisbury, showcasing findings that detail the earliest evidence of human occupation in the area, and other collections continue the story through the medieval period up to the Victorians.

Nearby, Mompesson House is a wonderful example of a Queen Anne period residence, dating from the early 18th century. The house was used to film part of the 1995 Ang Lee film *Sense and Sensibility*. We've met some very early residents of the house in the cathedral – though it was completely remodelled by their descendants. Check out the amazing sweeping carved staircase and ornate plaster-work ceilings.

Film fans will appreciate a trip to Wilton House, about 2 miles west of the city. One of the most famous stately houses in the country and still the home of the earls of Pembroke, it has featured in *The Madness of King George* and *Pride and Prejudice*, as well as *Sense and Sensibility*. There are lots of treasures to admire here, from frescoed ceilings to period furniture and artworks by van Dyck and Rembrandt, as well as the wonderful gardens, largely created by Capability Brown.

Stonehenge is, of course, one of the country's most famous and iconic historical sites and within easy distance of Salisbury. The stone circle is at least 5,000 years old and still a source of complete fascination – with all of its whys, hows and whos. Unless you pay to access the visitor centre you can only look at the stones from a distance, but even your admission fee won't get you inside the magical stone circle. However, the pathway around the edge gets you very close to it.

Also outside Salisbury, about 2 miles north of the city, is the site of Old Sarum. Today its ramparts sit on a grass-covered hill and it's hard to imagine that it was once one of the most important towns in this part of the country. The original stone foundations of Salisbury's early cathedral are still visible here, as is the spire of the new one.

If you want to wake up to a view of that spire, check yourself into the Rose and Crown, a wonderful 13th-century coaching inn with riverside gardens that offer beautiful views of the water meadows and cathedral. It's wonderfully atmospheric with olde-world timber beamed interiors, alongside modern light-filled conservatory spaces. Old style rooms are available in the main house, there is also a contemporary bedroom extension.

Chapter 3

Wells

Beside the great spring called 'Wiela'

Wells Cathedral. (© *Bernadette Fallon*)

It was a Roman mausoleum in the 5th century and the Church of Aldhelm in the 8th. It was a cathedral in 909, though subsequently lost its status for nearly 200 years. The present building was started in the 12th century, and the magnificent west front, the first part of the cathedral that most people see, is decorated with one of the largest collections of medieval statues in Europe. Though the days when it was a beacon of colour, covered in bright reds, blues and greens and alive with song as the voices of choristers and the sounds of trumpets rang out between the statues, are long gone.

The holy springs that give Wells its name have attracted pilgrims to the city for almost 2,000 years. You can still see the four springs today and it's a good place to start your cathedral visit, in the cannery garden that was once the site of the building's Lady Chapel. At the end of the garden, through a pretty arched opening, the well of St Andrew is visible in the grounds of the bishop's palace next-door.

It's thought that the King of Wessex gave the land to the abbot Aldhelm to build a church in 705 on the site of what was most probably an earlier place of Roman worship. Sixty years later, according to local records, more royal land was given 'to the Minster beside the great spring called Wiela that the priests there may more diligently serve only God in the church of St Andrew the Apostle'.

In 909, that church became a cathedral and so it remained until after the arrival of William the Conqueror. William replaced many of the local Saxon bishops with his own Norman men across the country, but Wells already had a French bishop, Bishop Giso of Lorraine, who remained until his death in 1088. After that, John of Tours took up the position in Wells.

He didn't stay long. Deciding that Bath, a more central location with an established reputation as a place of medical healing, was more suitable to a man of his status – he was also a physician – he moved his bishopric there. Wells didn't manage to re-establish its status as a cathedral until 1245, after the building of the mighty west front.

By then the building had moved from the original Saxon church to a site just north of it. Today's building was started around 1175 by Bishop de Bohun, another Frenchman, built in the Gothic style of architecture popular in France at the time. In fact, Wells was one of the first cathedrals in the UK to be built entirely in the Gothic style. Not only that, it features all three phases of Gothic, so it is possible to see how the style evolves, from Early English to Decorated to Perpendicular.

But there are also links between old and new. The cathedral font was transferred from the original Saxon building, so today's baptisms continue the legacy of Christian christenings here for over 1,000 years. Although the font now has a 'new' 17th-century cover.

Look closely at the font to see its 'modernisations'. The arches around the side are damaged where the stonemasons tried to make the rounded Saxon arches more pointed in the new Gothic style. There are

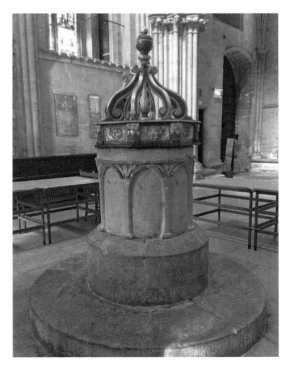

Wells font.
(© *Bernadette Fallon*)

traces in the stone where sculptures have been removed and the text encircling the top has also been destroyed – clearly too 'Saxon' to have survived, a blight on 'modern' 12th-century sensibilities.

Staying in the garden for a moment, consider that you are standing on the site of what was once a Lady Chapel. It was demolished during the 16th-century Reformation, when a member of the local gentry was told he could have its timbers, lead and masonry for his own use. And to get at them, he blew the chapel up. Excavations carried out on the building in the 20th century uncovered holes in the bottom of the pillars where the explosives were placed.

Out here, the scars of old doors are also visible, dating back to the building's very foundation and now blocked in for centuries. Building was carried out in the warmer months and in winter, work stopped with the walls covered to protect them from the elements. But the church was still used for worship, even as it was being built, so doors were created as needed and blocked off later as the building progressed and new entrances were opened.

Nearby, the cloisters enclose the palm churchyard, the burial place for cathedral clergy. Look out for the 'dipping place', leading down to the water flowing through a conduit under the cloisters, from the wells to the town. In the 15th century, the cloisters were re-modelled to build the upper storeys to house the library and choir schoolroom. Over 6,000 books are kept in the library, with the earliest dating from the 16th century.

Curious facts: the importance of the scissor arches

Moving inside the cathedral, the nave is a marvel of Gothic space, with its pointed arches, ceiling vaults and large windows flooding the interior with light. Along the sides the beautiful triforium arches draw the eye towards the quire screen and great scissor arches at the east end. Striking the scissor arches may be, but their function is more important than this. They were created to stop the central tower falling down.

In 1313, an elaborate extension and lead cap spire had added substantial extra weight to the top of the central tower with dire consequences – it started to crack and lean. So between 1338 and 1348, master mason William Joy erected a scissor arch on each of three sides of the crossing under the tower, designed to redistribute the tower's weight and, along with hidden buttresses, provide support. And it's stayed solidly in place ever since.

Look closely at the nave. Does it remind you of anything? With its tall pillars drawing the eye up to the exquisitely carved foliage

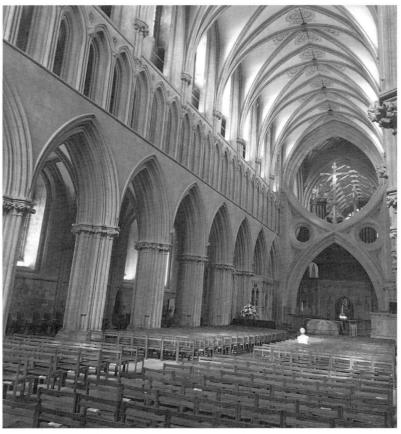

Wells nave. (© *Bernadette Fallon*)

erupting at the top of the columns, the nave appears to have been created as an avenue of trees, drawing the eye to the high altar. Either side, three levels of arches point straight up to heaven.

Don't miss: sad Adam Lock

An earlier master mason, Adam Lock, is immortalised in the nave, close to the entrance. High up on a pillar, his mournful face looks out towards the great west door. He started as an apprentice when the building work began, rising through the ranks to master mason as work moved towards the west end and completion, the life of the church mapping his own.

But why so mournful?

He died before the west end was completed and his stone face gazes forever at the part of the cathedral he was destined never to see. Instead, the deputy mason who became his successor, Thomas Norreys, oversaw the decoration of the mighty west front.

Around the cathedral, many pillars burst forth with decorated ornamentation and you can trace the progression of the masons from newly trained novices to masters of their craft as the stories told in stone become more elaborate with experience. There is a wonderful story of a grape-theft told through carvings on four sides of a pillar, from the deed to discovery to punishment, complete with dramatic expressions and expressive gestures. There's even a hat being knocked off by an angrily thrusted pitchfork. The carvings date from 1190 and demonstrate how storytelling was brought to life from paintings on flat walls into glorious physical relief.

You'll find many fascinating details on the pillars, such as the man with a toothache, pulling his jaw wide to demonstrate his pain. He's on a column close to the tomb of William Byton, just outside the quire. Byton was believed to have the cure for toothache – say his name out loud and you'll realise how fitting this is – and in fact his gravestone had to be covered over in the Middle Ages for protection.

Pillar carving.
(© *Bernadette Fallon*)

So many visitors were touching it to receive the cure that it was being slowly eroded. Byton was Bishop of Wells from 1266 to 1274 and when his body was exhumed, it was reported he was found with his full set of teeth intact.

In some places you will see traces of medieval paint, dating back to the time the cathedral was brightly coloured and decorated in primary red ochre. There are also fragments of brightly coloured paint on a few tombs, including William of March. He was once the resident 'saint in waiting' here. Unlike other cathedrals, Wells did not have a saint to bring in pilgrims and, more importantly, their money, so the pope was heavily petitioned to canonise William. He eventually said no and William's tomb was moved into a corner, no longer of any use.

The ceiling design in the nave is eye-catching but not medieval. It was added by the Victorians, though it was based on a design from the Middle Ages. Back then there would have been up to fifty chantry chapels in the church. Today just two remain, right at the top of the nave. These are dedicated to Bishop Bubwith, who gave money not only for his own chapel but for the almshouses and library that still exist today in the city, and to Dr Hugh Sugar, the keeper of the treasures and a stand-in for bishops. Created in the mature flowering of the Gothic style, these chapels represent the full flourishing of design intricacies and details of the period.

Don't miss: the mistake in the pulpit

Nearby, the Renaissance pulpit, created the following century, is simple and classic. Its only decoration is a text inscription from the *Cloverdale Bible*, the first to be published after the Reformation, though there is quite a comical mistake that somewhat spoils its classical elegance – if you know where to look. Follow the text right to the end and there, around a corner against a pillar, the sculptor ran out of space so instead of referencing 'Timothy' at the end of the line, it now refers to 'Timo'.

Moving closer to the quire, you'll find an ancient link with the original cathedral building that this one replaces. Outside the sacred quire walls, the holiest part of the building, are the tombs of seven previous bishops. The youngest dates back to 1088, Bishop Giso of Lorraine, who was in place before the coming of William the Conqueror.

Curious facts: the merging of 'two quires'

The quire was the first part of the cathedral to be completed and was probably in use before 1200. Between 1320 and 1340 it was extended eastwards to join the existing Lady Chapel. So today it is double the size it once was, but the extension was carried out with such sensitivity and skill that it is easy to miss the fact it was created in two separate parts in entirely different centuries. Though there are clues. The tabernacles, which are an architectural feature of the later period, can be seen in the second half of the quire, nearest to the Lady Chapel. The original Gothic arches in the top part of the quire have been 'tabernacled' to match, but they are not quite as ornate. However, the Lierne vaulting of the later extension was carried through the whole space to give unity and is a fine example of this type of work.

In the wooden stalls you'll find wonderful misericords, the 'mercy seats' for the clergy to lean against, carved from single pieces of oak, all telling their fantastical stories of humans, animals and mythical figures. These were added in the second period of quire building and the cathedral still has the bill for them – dated 1335. There was, in fact, some dispute over the payment and in the end it appears that the individual canons had to pay for their own seats. The stone cathedra – the bishop's throne that gives a cathedral its name and distinguishes it from a church – also dates from this period and is one of the few made from stone that still exists in the country, most others being wooden.

The decorative embroideries that hang behind the seats of the choir were carried out from 1937 and mainly completed during the Second World War, created by ninety-three women of the parish and seven men. Here you'll see a cardinal's hat, intended to represent King Henry VIII's right-hand man until he fell from favour just before the Reformation – a Reformation he was partly responsible for. After he failed to get the pope to agree to Henry's divorce from Catherine of Aragon, Henry nominated himself head of the church and granted his own divorce. That man was Cardinal Wolsey, who was in fact once Bishop of Bath & Wells, though the position was made only 'in commendam' – in trust while the role was vacant.

The Reformation wreaked considerable damage on the cathedral and the Lady Chapel was completely destroyed. Today's chapel contains some of the original glass from the 14th century, alongside a jumble of fragments saved from the Civil War in the 1600s. There was more damage to come. During the 17th-century Monmouth rebellion, when James, Duke of Monmouth and illegitimate son of Charles II, attempted to overthrow James II, troops stationed themselves in the cathedral and stabled their horses in the nave. The cathedral reredos was hacked away and today, poignantly, it still stands as it was left, ornate stone carving against bare wall and empty plinths where statues once stood.

Don't miss: the Jesse window

They didn't destroy the magnificent Jesse window though, the great east window of the quire that dates from 1340. Why? Maybe because it was simply too difficult to reach. Whatever the reason, today it's thought to be one of the most splendid displays of 14th-century glass in the world. Known as the golden window, because of its colours that glow in the rising sun, it shows Christ's family tree from Jesse, the father of King David.

Take time to look at the Cope chest in the retrochoir, the oldest dated piece of furniture in the country. Its origins are believed to be about 1120, and as the current building wasn't started until 1175, it's likely this chest came from the original Saxon cathedral. Today it holds important church possessions, but due to its great age is not opened every day.

Wells' magnificent chapter house, for which it is justly famous, was completed in 1306 after the restoration of the building to cathedral status. It is reached by a regal flight of steps curving up to the right, with another section of stairs continuing straight ahead to the Chain Gate Bridge that leads to Vicars Hall. This section was added in the 15th century and runs high across the road into Vicars Close.

The staircase windows hold the oldest stained-glass in the cathedral, dating from 1290. Look out for the small carved man on

Chapter house staircase. (© *Bernadette Fallon*)

the wall as you ascend the steps, fighting a dragon at his feet with one hand while casually holding up a pillar with the other.

The octagonal chapter house is a wonderful example of the Decorated Gothic style of architecture and features a central pillar supporting a vaulted roof, the ribs radiating from the pillar

Wells Chapter house. (© *Bernadette Fallon*)

resembling a mighty fountain in the centre of the room. The roof
is technically known as a tierceron vault, which is not a fan vault,
though the fan vault did develop from it. Most of the windows
were smashed in the 17th century destruction, but some of the
original medieval glass survived in the tracery lights, higher up.

Legend has it that the little carved heads over each stall represent real characters alive at the time of building, though there are no historical traces of Wells ever simultaneously having ten bishops, not to mention six popes.

The canons' seats are marked by individual nameplates on the wall, the vicars – who were their deputies – sat on the lower seats beneath. Today the full cathedral chapter only meets here on ceremonial occasions. And always without the bishop – through a quirk of history. In 1319, a power struggle between the dean and bishop of the day saw the bishop banished from the chapter house and since that day he hasn't been back. In the chapter house and cathedral the dean presides, while the diocese is the preserve of the bishop. And so the tradition continues.

Don't miss: the famous clock

The clock at Salisbury Cathedral may be five years older, but it doesn't have a face, so the clock at Wells is the oldest complete clock in the country. And what a marvel of engineering and artistry it is. Dating from the end of the 14th century, it is beautifully put together and still intact. Its face features a twenty-four-hour clock, a minute counter, the days of the month and the number of days since the last new moon. At each quarter hour, four jousting knights on horseback ride around a tower above the clock face and one is struck down – repeatedly – as they ride. Beside the clock, Jack Blandifer on the right-hand side, strikes bells at the hours and quarters with his heels, striking the bell in front of him with a hammer on the hour.

And that's not all. On the outside wall the entertainment continues with another clock dial and two knights working off the same interior mechanism, though this face dates from the 15th century. Here two knights strike the quarter hours on two bells. The clock's original medieval mechanism was replaced in 1837 and can now be seen in London's Science Museum.

The clock at Wells. (© *Bernadette Fallon*)

Take a look back at the great west front once more as you leave. It may have one of the finest collections of medieval statues in Europe but one of them looks slightly out of place. And it is. High above, looking down on the magnificent vista, sits Christ in Majesty, carved in 1985 to replace the fallen original.

Visiting Wells cathedral

Entry to Wells Cathedral is free, though donations are welcomed to help with the building's upkeep. Free tours run regularly and special interest tours are scheduled at intervals throughout the year. For more information visit Wellscathedral.org.uk.

Wells: where to go and what to do

Leave the cathedral by the north door and cross the road to reach the entrance into Vicars Close, thought to be the oldest complete medieval street in western Europe. It was built on the orders of Bishop Ralph of Shrewsbury in the 14th century to provide accommodation for the Vicars Choral, who sang every day in the cathedral. Forty-two houses were built, one per vicar – one room downstairs, one room upstairs – though some were merged after the Reformation when vicars were allowed to marry. The iconic chimneys were added in the 15th century to raise the smoke away from the houses and prevent it interfering with the important vocal cords housed within. Today there are twenty-seven houses in the close, still accommodating all twelve men of the choir, the organists and vergers.

On the other side of the cathedral grounds, the grand bishop's palace, complete with moat, is one of the oldest inhabited buildings in England, dating from the 13th century. Home to the Bishop of Bath & Wells since that time, its state rooms, ruined great hall and the bishop's private chapel are all open to the public. As are the fourteen acres of gardens outside – check out the resident swans in the moat who ring a bell when they want food, a tradition that has continued for the last 150 years. Here you'll also find the famous holy springs that give the city its name.

You might not be able to stay in a vicar's or bishop's house when you visit Wells, but you can wake up just as close to the cathedral as they do. The Swan Hotel, dating back to the 15th century, is located opposite the cathedral, which means some of its hotel bedrooms have uninterrupted views of the magnificent west front. This former posting house was once where horses were kept for the use of medieval travellers. Today, as well as sumptuous four poster beds, period features inside include heavy ceiling beams and panelling, while open fires with stone surrounds make this cosy hotel an inviting place to relax. Its more contemporary history includes hosting cast members of the UK film *Hot Fuzz*, filmed around Wells in 2006.

Wells is England's smallest city and very easy to explore on foot. Around the cathedral are atmospheric cobbled streets and medieval buildings, and here too you'll find the city's centuries-old market place within attractive 15th-century gateways. Markets take place twice a week.

The Wells & Mendip Museum offers information on the cathedral's architecture, as well as local life and the famous Witch of Wookey Hole. Wookey Hole is the name given to the limestone caverns on the edge of the Mendip Hills, 3 miles outside the city. The 'witch' is one of the many stalagmites and stalactites inside the caverns, changed from her human form by a local priest.

Enjoy another natural landscape phenomenon at Cheddar Gorge, the limestone cliffs created during the last Ice Age that are England's deepest natural canyon. Under the cliffs you can explore a few of the caves, or access the deep underground by signing up for a caving tour. There's a bracing 3-mile clifftop trail with spectacular views over the gorge, accessed by Jacob's Ladder, a 274-step climb.

As well as having a gorge, Cheddar is also famously the home of some very popular cheese. At the Cheddar Gorge Cheese Company you can take a tour of the cheese-making facilities and, obviously, buy cheese. Cheddar cheese has been produced here since the 12th century and Henry II, apparently, was a very big fan.

Glastonbury is within easy access of Wells, with its fascinating ruined abbey and mystical tor. It's famous the world over for its music festival but its spiritual history has been drawing visitors for centuries and the tor, which is another name for a rocky peak, was an important Pagan site. Surrounded in legend, the site is said to be both home of the king of the underworld as well as the mystic Isle of Avalon where King Arthur is buried. Topped by the ruined medieval Chapel of St Michael, the trail to the summit of the tor is half-an-hour's walk. The nearby abbey was dissolved during the time of the Reformation and fell into ruin. But you can still see the thorn bush, said to have sprung from the staff of Joseph of Arimathea, the man responsible for the burial of Jesus Christ, when he visited the abbey after the crucifixion.

The nearest mainline rail stations to Wells are Bristol and Bath with excellent connections to London and the south. Both are located about thirty-five minutes drive-time from Wells and run regular bus services to the city.

Chapter 4

Gloucester

From royal abbey to magical cloisters

Gloucester Cathedral. (*Photo by Angelo Hornak:* © *Gloucester Cathedral*)

It has crowned a king and buried a king and is one of only six former abbeys refounded as cathedrals after Henry VIII closed all the others during the Reformation. And it's considered one of the finest examples of the Perpendicular Gothic style in all of Britain. But if Westminster Abbey claims to have crowned every monarch since William the Conqueror, who's telling lies?

We shall see.

Gloucester was a royal borough in the Middle Ages and the site of an Anglo–Saxon palace, which today is beneath the local Kingsholm

St Kyneburga. (© *Bernadette Fallon*)

rugby ground. After his arrival, William the Conqueror continued Gloucester's royal privileges, holding a crown-wearing service in the city every Christmas to re-enact his Westminster Abbey coronation. He also restored the fortunes of Gloucester Abbey, installing the acclaimed Norman abbot Serlo to make it one of the greatest Benedictine abbeys in England.

The monastery was founded in 679 by Osric, a Mercian prince, and his sister Kyneburga was its first abbess. A statue in the cathedral carved by its modern-day master mason, Paschal Mychalysin, in 2013 is testament to how, despite outward appearances, women frequently played a strong part in the life of the church in the Middle Ages. As they frequently do today. Gloucester Cathedral was the first to appoint a diocesan female bishop, Rachel Treweek, in 2015.

But by the time the Normans arrived in the 11th century, the monastery was in poor repair. Building on the new Norman structure started in the east end in 1100 under its new bishop, Serlo. Today's cathedral has strong Norman features but also many elements of the later Gothic style, and could be described as a Norman building given a Gothic makeover.

Fires in the nave destroyed the early timber ceiling – twice – leading to its replacement with the fine stone vaulting you see today. In fact, Gloucester has beautiful examples of all types of vaulting throughout the building, particularly in the cloisters that erupt in a cascade of exquisite patterning – a feature of the high Perpendicular style for which the cathedral is known.

We may have just one man to thank for that. And that's the dead king who is buried here. Or, more correctly, his son.

Edward II was a very unpopular king. The son of Edward I, a king who had been known as 'most victorious', the second Edward was nothing of the kind. In fact, his defeat by Robert the Bruce and the Scots at Bannockburn has been described as probably the worst medieval military disaster in British history.

Gloucester nave. (© *Bernadette Fallon*)

But it wasn't only that. His close relations with, and excessive promotion of, certain – male – favourites in the royal court didn't win him any fans either. He spent so much time ensconced with one of his male courtiers after his wedding to Queen Isabella, that she went back home to France. His rule saw famines and executions, unrest and dissention. When finally Isabella returned with an army, which included her lover Roger Mortimer, Edward's enemies rose up against him and he was imprisoned in Berkeley Castle in Gloucester.

It's not known how he died or who killed him, but an unpopular, deposed, imprisoned king is never going to be very safe. He died in September 1327, and the official line is that he suffocated. But he is also reported to have been 'sleyne with a hoot broche putte thro the secrete place posterialle' – or, in more contemporary language, a hot poker up his rear end. This was presumably in revenge for his rumoured indiscretions, though it should be pointed out he had two sons and two daughters with Isabella, and an illegitimate son before his marriage.

He was buried in Gloucester Abbey in 1327 and while his enemies might have wished for him to fade quickly from memory, he wasn't forgotten by his son. Edward III was crowned at the age of just 14, and by the time he reached 17 he had killed his mother's lover, banished her into exile and avenged his father's death. He went on to become one of the most powerful and respected kings in history, restoring the country's military fortunes and ruling for fifty years.

He also deftly remodelled great swathes of the interior at Gloucester with the intention – one presumes – of making it fit to be the final resting place of a king. It's said that his royal master masons were despatched to the cathedral to carry out his wishes, and the architectural style here after their arrival became grander and more refined.

The south transept, remodelled from about 1331, is the earliest surviving example of Gothic Perpendicular in England. The ceiling work is quite magnificent and the increased size of the enlarged windows casts light on the delicate lattice work to illuminate it even further. This part of the cathedral is the oldest surviving example of the English Perpendicular style.

The tomb of Edward II is located in some splendour close to the altar, as befits the tomb of a king. It's thought to have been designed and commissioned by his son in the 1330s and has been described as one of the finest canopy tombs in the country. Under the canopy, you can see the workings of the fine miniature vaulting inside. It is the first royal effigy to be carved in alabaster and the limestone base is covered in Purbeck marble. It is also one of the few monarch's tombs to be located outside London. A stained-glass window by Clayton Bell in the south aisle commemorates Edward's burial.

It's believed that the tomb was a place of pilgrimage for many years after Edward's death, though he was never canonised a saint. Not that there weren't efforts in this direction. His great-grandson, King Richard II, who ruled England from 1377 to 1399, asked the Bishop of London to intercede with Pope Boniface IX to have Edward canonised. In 1394, the pope was sent a book of miracles that Edward was supposedly responsible for – along with some lavish gifts – but nothing came of it. The pope was apparently not convinced.

Tomb of Edward II.
(© *Bernadette Fallon*)

Richard had earlier moved his royal parliament to Gloucester, following serious unrest in London. The king stayed in the abbey and the court business was conducted in the chapter house. Were they drawn by the presence of a king – albeit a dead one? Perhaps. The dead king may also have been responsible for another – much more important – event. An event that saved the abbey from destruction. After Henry VIII's dissolution of the monasteries, most religious houses were destroyed and dispossessed. But Gloucester Abbey was one of only six to survive. Dissolved as a monastery, yes. But now granted new cathedral status, it was allowed to continue. Did Henry feel some kinship with his ancestor and decide to preserve the building?

In a time when Edward II was reviled and plotted against, even by his own wife and mother of his children, the tomb can be seen as a tribute of love. A tribute of love by his son who, despite the opinion of nobles and the court, made a grand statement with his work in Gloucester Cathedral to honour his father and restore the prestige of the monarchy.

Curious facts: the body in the tomb

But is it the king's body at all in the tomb? Or did he escape to end his remaining days as a hermit in Italy? In Languedoc in France there is a copy of a letter addressed to King Edward III by Manuele Fieschi, an important papal official. This official says he wants to tell the king that he has met a man claiming to be Edward II, who described the specific details of his escape from Berkeley Castle. According to the letter, Edward was warned he was about to be killed by his guard and so escaped by killing the gate porter and stealing his keys.

He first made his way to Ireland, then France. He was received by the pope, then taking on the guise of a hermit, he went to Germany and ended his days in Italy, where he wrote down his confession for Fieschi. But why should it be given any credibility? Well, the man who wrote the original letter was a respected official in the pope's employment. But not only that, the original letter was said to carry the king's royal seal.

But if that's the case, just who is in the tomb? It definitely contains a body as it was exhumed in the 19th century. The theory goes that the knights sent to kill Edward covered up his escape by putting the body of the gate porter, killed by the king, into his coffin instead. So, for all these centuries have pilgrims to the king's tomb been paying homage to a porter?

Don't miss: the magnificent quire

The royal patronage of Edward III was also responsible for the Perpendicular remodelling of the quire in the 14th century. His masons removed the existing roof and demolished the east end, then raised the walls and created a stunning lierne vault. New quire stalls were added and fitted with fifty-eight misericords and their carvings. Today, forty-six are the medieval originals, while the remainder are Victorian.

In place of the previous east end, a vast new window was constructed, which is today the second largest medieval stained-glass church window in Britain, with at least seventy percent of its original glass still intact. At the time of its installation in the 1350s, it was the biggest window in the world. It measures the size of a tennis court – 72 feet high and 38 feet wide.

It's believed that the glass – richly coloured in many shades of reds and blues and, thus, very expensive – came from Rouen. Among the many depictions it shows are abbots, bishops and kings, saints, martyrs and apostles, the shields of the noblemen who fought in battle with Edward III, and Mary and Jesus at its centre. And a golfer.

A golfer?

Well, he certainly looks like a golfer, poised with his club at the far corner of the right-hand side of the window. However, as golf was not invented until the following century, it is safe to say he is playing a different – though very similar – ball game. But why is he in a window, among such illustrious company? Nobody knows. But you can buy a postcard of him in the cathedral shop to take home for contemplation.

Outside the quire in the south transept, look up to see a rather unique stone carving suspended from a bracket on the wall. Featuring a mason with his apron of tools, it dates to the mid-1300s and was thought to be a memorial to the mason's son. This, presumably, is the figure shown falling through the air as the mason watches, mouth open in disbelief. A memorial to some grisly accident that occurred during the building of the cathedral, then?

This was the original interpretation of the carving for many centuries. But a recent art historian visitor to the cathedral disagreed. The Professor of Medieval Art History from Cambridge pointed out a few salient facts. First, this is a holy part of the cathedral, a memorial to a mere mason would never have been displayed here. Second, the boy is not represented falling in the conventional manner. Falling in medieval depictions was quite simple. It happened head first, feet in the air. Here the boy is upright, while his hand is grazing the wall.

So, what if this records not a tragedy but a miracle? The boy starts to fall but the flight is arrested and he is saved. Below, his father the mason is open-mouthed not in horror but in wonder. It is certainly a happier interpretation of this interesting artwork.

Curious facts: the stories of the tombs

Edward II is not the only interesting tomb to be found in Gloucester, even regardless of the fact he may be a 14th-century porter. Near him lies Osric, who we met earlier at the foundation of the abbey. He's the Prince of Mercia who together with his sister, the first abbess Kyneburga, was responsible for the first religious settlement on the site. He died in the 8th century, so his tomb should be well weathered and worn. But it looks pristine. Another miracle?

Not a miracle, just some effective political wrangling by the monks who wanted to preserve their abbey. It is not a tomb, but a memorial, built in the turbulent days leading up to the dissolution of the monasteries in the hope that the presence of another royal personage would persuade the king of the abbey's importance, and spare it.

There is another royal connection in the cathedral. And not just the controversial crowning of a king outside the traditional coronation site of Westminster Abbey. We'll come to that later. This concerns another tomb.

It's believed that the son of one of the most famous kings of England is buried in the chapter house at Gloucester. His memorial can be seen on the south side of the cathedral. Robert, Duke of Normandy, was given the duchy after the death of his father, William the Conqueror, in 1087. The second son, who received England, may have got the better deal and was crowned William II. The third son received a large amount of silver and the squabbling between them began. When William II was killed while out hunting – interestingly, a death foreseen by a monk in Gloucester Abbey – his younger brother Henry seized the throne, invaded Normandy and held his older brother Robert prisoner in England for the rest of his life. Robert died eventually in Cardiff Castle.

Don't miss: the famous cloisters

The cloisters are one of the glories of Gloucester, famous for their wonderful fan vaulting and in fact the first known example of vaulting on this scale. They date from the second half of the 14th century and were completed in the early years of the 15th century. They have inspired many copies, among them Bath and Kings College Cambridge.

Today the cloisters are also famous for another reason. These magical walkways became the equally magical corridors of Hogwarts School of Witchcraft and Wizardry in the first two Harry Potter films, *Harry Potter and the Philosopher's Stone* and *Harry Potter and*

Gloucester cloisters. (© *Bernadette Fallon*)

the Chamber of Secrets by J.K. Rowling. They have also been used for filming *Sherlock*, *Wolf Hall* and *Doctor Who*.

But long before Harry and his friends learned the art of wizardry at Gloucester, the monks used the space for their own studies. You can still the carrels along the south walk – the arched spaces with windows – where their desks would have rested. Along the west end of the north walk is the lavatorium, where they washed. It's also where Harry Potter and Ron Weasley hide from a giant troll in *Harry Potter and the Philosopher's Stone*.

The cloisters may be beautiful but, for a monk working diligently at his manuscripts, also very draughty. So, in the 15th century, once the library was built, their desks were moved here for comfort, placed by the north window to avail of the gentle light. Due to the size of the library, it's likely it was also an educational space and, in fact, it was legally established as one after the abbey was dissolved. When Henry VIII re-founded Gloucester as a cathedral, he established a school in the library. King's School still exists today, though it has long since moved from its original home.

The library has endured many ups and downs over the centuries, surviving a fire, the Civil War, and the eventual loss of the school. Today it's a fascinating treasure trove of books and history, and guided tours are available for a small fee. Or you can visit for free on public open days throughout the year. It holds manuscripts from the 12th century and books from the 15th century, but the oldest holding in the library dates back to Anglo-Saxon times – seven pieces of parchment telling the partial stories of the lives of the saints.

Among its most fascinating possessions are the books that date back to the time the library was a school, between 1684 and 1712, with notes written in the back by the headmaster. *Aesop's Fables* even has some 'extra' fables, the ones written by hand by the pupils themselves, which are often quite bawdy and full of schoolboy humour.

There are two more places to visit before you leave, at both ends of the spectrum: the crypt and the tower. The crypt is the oldest part of the building, dating from 1089, and it's here you will see the earliest Norman work in the cathedral. Watch out for the interesting wall full of carvings of various quality, which is likely to have been a place of practice for apprentices.

Building of the current tower was started under Abbot Seabroke in 1450 and finished in 1460, the third tower to be built at Gloucester. There are 269 steps to the top but there are four places to stop and catch your breath. These 'breathing spaces' also give a rare opportunity to see behind the scenes at the cathedral, from the south transept roof space where the techniques employed by medieval builders are evident, to the ringing chamber and belfry with its mighty bells. And finally, you step out on to the roof itself with its stunning views over the Severn Valley, Forest of Dean, Malvern Hills and the Cotswolds. Also from up here you can see the long line of solar panels on the roof of the nave below. The cathedral reportedly has more solar panels than any other medieval building in the world.

But what of that final royal connection, the king crowned in the cathedral? That story takes us back to the nave where we started. Here you'll find the 19th-century window that commemorates the coronation of Henry III, the son of King John, in this very building.

Henry was crowned at the age of just 9, during the tumultuous Civil War that followed John's renunciation of *Magna Carta*. The barons he fought had taken control of London, and Prince Louis of France was also holed-up there, hoping to take the throne of England that the barons had promised him. And so, with London closed to them, Henry's supporters had him quickly crowned in Gloucester, where the boy was living at the time.

In the absence of a crown – that too was in London – he was crowned using his mother's gold bracelet, clearly depicted in the stained-glass window. But Westminster Abbey is not incorrect to claim it has crowned every monarch since William the Conqueror (with a caveat). Because once Louis agreed to a truce and was paid to leave the country, Henry was eventually crowned again in Westminster.

What's the caveat?

Two kings of England have never been crowned at all. Edward VIII because he abdicated in 1936 before his coronation and, many centuries earlier, Edward V, because he was stripped of his title before he could be crowned. After his uncle claimed that the young king was illegitimate because his parents' marriage was invalid, Edward simply disappeared and his uncle was crowned instead. And that uncle? Richard III, the former Duke of Gloucester.

Visiting Gloucester Cathedral

There is no charge to enter Gloucester Cathedral and the cloisters, although donations are welcomed. Guides are available in the cathedral and it is possible to pre-book tours. There is a small fee for tours of the crypt and tower. For full details visit the website at Gloucestercathedral.org.uk.

Gloucester: where to go and what to do

The city started life as a Roman settlement but for centuries has been famous for its cathedral. It's the county capital of Gloucestershire and an excellent base for visiting the glorious surrounding countryside, from the Forest of Dean to the Cotswolds.

Gloucester was originally a Colonia, the highest-ranking type of provincial town in the Roman Empire, founded for retired members of the army. In total there were only four Colonia in Britain. Founded under the reign of Emperor Nerva, in around 98AD, today his statue sits on Southgate Street. The street follows the line of the original Roman road and extensive remains of the Roman forum still lie underneath it, near The Cross. This area has been an important commercial centre since the time of the Romans and Southgate Street was a busy trading area in the Middle Ages.

Get up close to some Roman ruins at the Eastgate viewing chamber, which displays the remains of defences dating back to the city's foundation. You'll also be able to see the foundations of a 13th-century tower and a Tudor horse pool, where wagons and livestock were cleaned up before being taken to market.

You can trace the important history of the city at the Museum of Gloucester through its medieval and Roman collections and, in fact, as far back as the Iron Age. The impressive Victorian building has recently been renovated. Also housed within the museum, its art collection includes works by J.M.W. Turner and Thomas Gainsborough.

For more specific historical collections, the Gloucester Life Museum tells the story of the city's history over several floors in an atmospheric old building. The Soldiers of Gloucestershire Museum is devoted to the history of the Gloucestershire Regiment – the most decorated regiment in the British Army – and their involvement in wars including the Napoleonic Wars and both world wars. Telling a more recent story, the Jet Age Museum is located close to where Britain's first jet aircraft was built, a short distance west of the city.

The historic Gloucester Docks have been extensively renovated and feature a fascinating insight into the workings of this important marine port. There are also plenty of places to shop, eat and drink, all set against the backdrop of this dramatic waterfront. Sections of the docks were recently used to shoot scenes from *Alice In Wonderland: Through the Looking Glass*. Gloucester Quays is a shopper's haven, with its converted warehouses now home to bargain outlets for many high end High Street brands.

Located in one of the Victorian warehouses at the docks, Gloucester Waterways Museum tells the story of the local canals and rivers, where visitors can climb aboard historic boats or experience the real thing outside. Boat trips along the Gloucester and Sharpness Canal and the River Severn feature historic commentaries along the way.

If you're visiting with Beatrix Potter fans, the Tailor of Gloucester Beatrix Potter Museum and Shop is located in the original building used by the writer in her story *The Tailor of Gloucester*.

A short distance from the city, Nature in Art is a museum and art gallery dedicated to art inspired by nature. It's worth the drive to see its location alone, the beautiful Georgian mansion Wallsworth Hall. Also outside the city, the Barn Owl Centre features owls, hawks, buzzards, falcons and golden eagles, where you can get up close to – and even handle – some of the birds.

In keeping with Gloucester's rich historical past, choose some very historic accommodation, right in the heart of the city and a short walk from the cathedral. The New Inn in Northgate Street was originally built as an inn for pilgrims visiting the shrine of King Edward II in St Peter's Abbey. It was rebuilt in 1455 as Gloucester became an important destination for the nobility and the inn became popular with visiting knights, yeomen and gentlemen. It also has a more tragic association with the ruling powers, as it was from the gallery of the inn that Lady Jane Grey was proclaimed Queen of England in 1553 by the Abbott of Gloucester. She ruled for only nine days and was eventually beheaded by the new monarch, Queen Mary. Today it's a fascinating example of a medieval galleried inn.

Chapter 5

Exeter

From Roman times to today

Exeter Cathedral. (© *Bernadette Fallon*)

The site of Exeter Cathedral has been a Christian place of worship since the Roman period. In its time it has been an Anglo–Saxon monastery that educated the county's most famous saint, a home for part of the true cross, and the site of a grisly murder. The cathedral that exists today was started by a nephew of William the Conqueror.

Though not much of it has lasted. The most obvious remains of that mighty Norman building from the 1100s are the solid twin towers, best appreciated from the green lawns that surround the cathedral. By the 1270s the Romanesque cathedral was being demolished to make way for a bigger, grander and much brighter Gothic building with magnificent architectural features. Today the Gothic stone vaulted ceiling at Exeter is the longest in the world.

Exeter was a fortified settlement in Roman times, though there is evidence that the city existed before this, settled by Cornish tribes. Regardless of who was here first, once the Romans left, an Anglo-Saxon monastery was built on the site where the cathedral now stands. St Boniface, a noble man from nearby Crediton who is credited with converting part of Germany to Christianity, studied here around 680. Athelstan, King of Wessex, refounded the monastery in 932, and it's likely it came under attack by the Vikings the following century.

The first Bishop of Exeter, Leofric, was installed in 1050 when King Edward the Confessor granted the cathedral's founding charter. Early records cite its formidable list of relics, including wood from Jesus' manger and pieces of his cross and tomb, fragments of bone from the apostles and some of the coal upon which St Laurence was roasted. But it wasn't until after William the Conqueror's victory at Hastings in 1066 that the current cathedral was started by one of his nephews, the new Bishop of Exeter, William Warelwast. And the reason the building lasted less than a century in its full Norman form may be due to its neighbour down the road in Wiltshire.

Salisbury Cathedral was consecrated in 1258 and heralded as one of the finest English Gothic cathedrals in the country. It is said that the then Bishop of Exeter, Bronescombe, became dissatisfied with Exeter's squat, dark Norman building after visiting Salisbury, and decided he would build his own Gothic cathedral. Exeter was completely remodelled except for the Norman towers – and even they had Gothic-shaped windows punched through them. Remarkably, the records detailing the rebuilding still survive from the late 13th century, one of the most complete set of accounts that exists for any cathedral in Europe.

The last part of the new cathedral to be completed is one of the first parts you will most likely see, the great west front and the cathedral's main entrance. It almost seems to come alive as you approach, with

The west front. (© *Bernadette Fallon*)

its screen of animated carved figures, rising in tiers from the ground. Heads are turned as if in conversation, arms are raised in gesture, this image screen is one of the finest examples of medieval sculpture in the country.

Interestingly, it was not part of the original cathedral design but an afterthought, believed to have been added after the then bishop,

Exeter nave vaulting. (© *Bernadette Fallon*)

Grandisson, saw the magnificent screen frontage of Wells Cathedral. The initial screen featured only two tiers, with angels on the bottom, knights and kings on top. The traces of paint that remain show that this was richly decorated in blues, golds and greens, on a background of red and green. Postcards on sale in the cathedral shop show a reconstruction of the west front with its magnificent paintwork.

A century later, the top tier of apostles was added either side of the central figures, which were probably created to represent Jesus Christ and the Virgin Mary. She didn't survive the Reformation purge though, and her place was filled by Richard II. At the top of the building, directly over the arched window, is a statue of St Peter, to whom the cathedral is dedicated – the Cathedral Church of Saint Peter at Exeter.

Inside, the cathedral shows the full flourishing of the Decorated period in all of its glory and is the only example in Europe of a Decorated Gothic building almost in its entirety. The cathedral nave is filled with light and the eye is drawn irresistibly upwards to the simply stunning stone vaulting, one of the glories of Exeter's architecture. The vaulting arches are locked in place by keystones, carved to create bosses, with the largest of these weighing over two tonnes. These bosses are intricately detailed with mythical creatures and monsters, mermaids, dragons and centaurs, alongside historical scenes such as the murder of Archbishop Thomas Becket in Canterbury Cathedral in 1170.

Curious facts: murder in the cathedral

Exeter Cathedral had its own murder 113 years later. In 1283, a bitter dispute arose between the man who wanted to be dean, John Pycot, and the bishop, Peter Quinil, who wasn't convinced. While the bishop was away, Pycot had himself elected by the cathedral chapter, much to the fury of Quinil. He refused to recognise the dean's election and instead made a man called Walter Lechlade precentor and head of the chapter, rendering Pycot's position irrelevant.

In November of that year, Lechlade was murdered as he walked to a service in the cathedral. While Pycot's involvement couldn't be proven, it was known that his associates had carried out the killing and the bishop appealed to King Edward I to come to Exeter to serve justice. The king spent Christmas at Rougemont Castle in the city and the trial lasted from Christmas Eve to 28 December. Several men, including the mayor of the city and the porter of the south gate, were found guilty and hanged.

Supporting the mighty nave ceiling, the pillars are made from Purbeck stone from nearby Dorset. Unlike other cathedrals, the stone is not polished to bring out its sheen but remains in a natural state with beautifully coloured textured bands of colour. Look up to see the minstrels' gallery, carved with a collection of angels playing medieval instruments. It's used at Christmas when the choir sing carols from here at evensong on Christmas Day.

Don't miss: the dog whipper's door

Nearby is the door to the dog whipper's apartment. These 'whippers' were employed in the cathedral from the 16th to the 19th centuries, both to remove stray dogs from the building and keep the ones that came in lawfully with their owners under control. Their kit included a special set of expanding tongs to reach dogs that had squeezed themselves into awkward-to-reach places.

Apparently, they were also required to clear the nave of peasants and traders whenever a cathedral procession was in progress and you can still see the glass windows halfway up the nave where they stood to keep an eye out for any recalcitrant – human or canine – for several centuries. It's thought that Exeter had one of the last ever dog whippers in the country, with the last appointment made in 1856.

But it's not all about dogs here. As you move around the cathedral you'll notice tributes and references to other animals too, from cats to elephants. The 'Exeter Elephant' has become very famous and is a 13th-century misericord carving that has been moved from its original place in the quire out to the north aisle so visitors can get a better view of it. It's thought to have been inspired by the elephant given as a gift to King Henry III by Louis IX of France, which was kept at the Tower of London. However, it's not quite clear if the craftsman who carved it actually saw the elephant. While the details of the body are largely correct – albeit with extremely ambitious tusks – the feet attached to the body resemble horses' hooves.

The cathedral holds one of the oldest complete sets of misericords in the country, carved in the 13th century and located in the quire. And, unlike the poor elephant, there are wonderfully lifelike animals carved in the choirstalls, which were designed by Sir George Gilbert Scott as part of his Victorian renovation. They were carved by the firm of Farmer and Brindley of London, who were reportedly

Quire carving.
(© *Bernadette Fallon*)

instructed to visit the Zoological Society in London – now London Zoo – to ensure they captured all of the details correctly.

The cathedra in the quire is one of the biggest in the country at 59 feet tall, and a particularly fine example of medieval woodwork, carved in the 14th century from a design by the master mason Thomas of Witney. This bishop's throne became the throne of a king-in-waiting in 1688 when it was occupied by Prince William of Orange in 1688 as his 'declaration of peaceful intent' was read.

William, the Dutch prince whose mother was the eldest daughter of King Charles II, was seen as a champion of the Protestant faith at a time when the English were fearful of a return to the old religion under the Catholic King James II. William, married to James' daughter Mary, was a strong contender for the throne. After landing at Torbay in Devon with his Dutch troops and making his 'declaration' in Exeter, he continued on to London, forcing King James to flee the country. William and Mary were crowned joint monarchs of England in April 1689 and of Scotland a month later. He is the last person in history to successfully invade England by force.

Look carefully at the pillars around the quire area and you'll find something a little bit surprising. Shrapnel damage. Large chunks of stone have been gouged out in several places and, if you look even closer, you'll see where two fingers were blown off, then replaced, on the effigy of Bishop Henry Marshall at the side of the quire.

What happened?

During the Second World War in May 1942, a bomb fell on the Chapel of St James in the south quire aisle, completely destroying it. One of the volunteer fire wardens, sheltering from the air-raid in the staircase leading to the dog whipper's room, wrote an account of the fateful night:

There was a whoosh that almost blew us up the stairs, a rumble of masonry and a tinkle of broken glass. The cautiously opened door revealed the cathedral brighter than ever with beams of light from the broken windows streaming through the dust. We made our way towards the south quire aisle… As we reached the gate we saw the dim light of the sky where the roof should have been and an immense pile of rubble topped by a section of the leaded roof.

In fact, the cathedral had a lucky escape – had the bomb fallen a few feet further in, it's likely the entire roof would have collapsed. Today the chapel has been completely rebuilt, a rare 20th-century addition to a medieval Gothic cathedral.

The fallout from the bomb had some interesting – and very unexpected – repercussions. When examining the building for bomb damage, several doll-sized wax figures were discovered hidden in the stonework above the tomb of Bishop Edmund Lacy, who died in 1455. Though Exeter didn't officially have a saint's grave, Lacy's came very close as medieval pilgrims were known to venerate the tomb of this very devout man. It's thought the pilgrims brought the figures to the tomb, representing themselves and the body parts they wanted healed, because as well as full figures, fragments of limbs were also discovered. They were probably hidden to save them from destruction during the Reformation.

Curious facts: the legacy of Bishop Oldham

There are several tombs and burial chapels in the quire aisles, including the chantry of Bishop Oldham in the Chapel of St Saviour. This holds his lasting legacy to the world – clear instructions on how to pronounce his name correctly. 'Oldham' is pronounced 'owl-dom' and the chapel is filled with carved owls as a reminder. And, lest there be any confusion, one of them is actually holding a banner that reads 'dom'. In his lifetime, the bishop founded Manchester Grammar School and was a founding benefactor of Corpus Christi College Oxford.

In the north aisle, you'll find a former Lord High Treasurer of England, Bishop of Exeter from 1308 to 1326, and another unfortunate link with murder. Walter de Stapledon had close connections to both kings Edward I and II, though being associated with the misdeeds and unpopularity of Edward II didn't do him any favours. Edward II was running for his life in 1326, as Queen Isabella of France approached London, intent on deposing him. He appointed the bishop keeper of the city but on his way to try to make peace between the warring factions, de Stapledon was ambushed. He fled to St Paul's seeking safety, but was dragged out by an angry mob to Cheapside. There his head was chopped off and his body thrown in a dunghill. His followers reburied it close to the River Thames but Queen Isabella later ordered it to be removed for burial to Exeter Cathedral, and so the bishop finally came home.

Walter de Stapledon was also responsible for founding Exeter College Oxford, which he set up to provide 'an educated clergy for his diocese'. Today it is more famous for its artistic alumni, who include the authors J.R. Tolkien, Alan Bennett and Philip Pullman, artist William Morris and actor Richard Burton.

Curious facts: the mystery of the armour

A peculiar discovery was recently made about the monument of Sir John Gilbert. The half-brother of Sir Walter Raleigh, he died in 1596 and his effigy, lying beside his wife, is depicted in full armour. Only it couldn't be his. A visiting expert to the cathedral said the armour is completely wrong for the period, pre-dating it by centuries. So, it looks like the head of Sir John was attached to another body to make his monument.

The largest chapel in the cathedral, as is usual, is the Lady Chapel and this is where the Gothic rebuilding began towards the end of the 13th century. It's full of light and colour, with its large stained-glass window featuring the Virgin Mary, quirky medieval wall carvings and

Gilbert tomb.
(© *Bernadette*
Fallon)

highly decorated roof bosses. These were repainted by Sir George
Gilbert Scott during his renovation of the cathedral. While he was
pleased with the work here, some of that carried out by his colleagues
nearby did not meet with his approval. Writing in his *Personal and
Professional Recollections* in 1879:

> *The decoration of the vaulting of the Lady Chapel is an exact
> restoration of what was found. In the side chapels, Mr. Clayton
> weakly departed from the old design, so far as to add some foolish
> patterns to the mouldings, otherwise it would have been correct.*

The effigy of Lady Dorothea Dodderidge here attracts a lot of interest from fashion students, dressed in its elaborate gown, trimmed with what is believed to be Honiton lace from Devon.

Lady Dodderidge tomb. (© *Bernadette Fallon*)

Don't miss: the dentist in the chapel

Nearby you'll find some unfortunate – and very prolific – examples of medieval graffiti, covering Bishop Stafford's alabaster effigy. The bishop died in 1419, the graffiti dates from the 1600s, though some of it may be as early as 1580. Close by is the Chapel of St Gabriel, with its striking image of St Apollonia on the door. She is the patron saint of dentists – and is she carrying what you think she's carrying? She is. An extracted tooth in a pair of pincers.

Close to the Lady Chapel lies Bishop Bronescombe, the man who started building the magnificent Gothic cathedral we see today, even though, by the time of his death, the east end of the cathedral and the Lady Chapel, the first sections to be built, were only half-finished. He died in 1280 and, remarkably, his effigy still retains its original colouring, over 800 years later.

And while you unfortunately won't be able to see it, there's more graffiti to be found in the organ loft, though this is of a more illustrious nature. Music lovers will be familiar with the wonderful Baroque compositions of Matthew Locke from the 17th century. Born in 1621, he was a composer for King Charles II, but was first a chorister at Exeter Cathedral. During recent restoration work in the organ loft, his name and the date were found carved deep in the parapet, his piece of 375-year-old schoolboy graffiti from 1638.

Don't miss: the cat in the transept

There's another small 'memorial' to another very famous animal in the cathedral's history, the cat employed from the 14th century to kill the mice and rats in the building. A hole cut in a door in the north transept is a sort of medieval cat flap and the cat itself was paid a penny a week for its trouble. The payment is entered in the cathedral

Medieval clock beside Precentor Sylke's tomb. (© *Bernadette Fallon*)

archives from 1305 to 1467 and was presumably used to supply the moggy's non-vermin diet.

Above it is the Exeter Astronomical Clock, which dates from 1484 and shows the time and the phases of the moon, with the sun and moon revolving around the earth. The phases of the moon were used to calculate the timing of Easter and also the cycle of the tides, very important to Exeter as a port town.

The clock proved very popular with the aforementioned mice, who were attracted to the ropes of the clock mechanism by the fat used as a lubricant. In fact, this is thought to be the origin of the well-known children's nursery rhyme:

Hickory, dickory, dock
The mouse ran up the clock
The clock struck one
The mouse ran down
Hickory, dickory, dock

Under the clock and beside the 'cat flap' door is the chantry chapel of Precentor Sylke, with its slightly gruesome cadaver tomb, showing the decaying corpse of this 15th-century clergyman. The legs are missing, presumably part of the Reformation destruction, but we get the message. This is our reminder that life is transient, quickly passing and our fate awaits us. In case we're in any way unsure, the tomb is inscribed with the words: 'I am what you will be, and I was what you are. Pray for me I beseech you.'

The north and south transepts have been created from the Norman towers, which had their inside walls removed to open them up to the cathedral crossing. Over in the south transept is the monumental memorial to the 14th-century Earl of Devon, Hugh de Courtenay, and his wife Margaret. An important family back then, their 20th-century descendants include Sir Winston Churchill.

And so the cycle continues here in the cathedral, from tales of power and prestige and medieval glory to the contemporary appeal it holds for the millions who still flock here to visit, to worship and to marvel.

de Courtenay tomb. (© *Bernadette Fallon*)

Visiting Exeter Cathedral

There is a fee to enter the cathedral outside of service times. Guided tours are free of charge and run several times during the day, or visitors can follow an audio tour, which is also free. For more information visit Exeter-cathedral.org.uk.

Exeter: where to go and what to do

The area around the cathedral is medieval Exeter at its best: winding cobbled streets and buildings that date from the Middle Ages alongside traces of the city's even older Roman past. And each historical settlement has left its mark – from the fragments of Roman city streets and fortified walls to the Norman cathedral towers and elegant Georgian homes. It has something for everybody: history, culture, a buzzing social life, good shopping – even a quayside where you can try your hand at canoeing.

Familiarise yourself with the city and enjoy a glimpse into its fascinating past on a free walking tour with a Red Coat Guide. There are several themed tours to choose from, depending on your interests, each one lasts ninety minutes and there's no need to book – just turn up.

For an indoor wander through history, head for the Royal Albert Memorial Museum & Art Gallery. From prehistory to the present, collections include Roman artefacts as well as exhibits from the ancient worlds, and the museum also tells the story of global exploration and of collecting itself.

Close to the cathedral, the underground passages are something a little bit different. These medieval passages formerly carried water around the city and now a tour around the underground warren offers a lively look into their previous history.

The Romans built a huge fortress in the city when they arrived in around AD55, including a 2-mile defensive wall. Part of this can still be seen in Rougemont Gardens. The gardens were originally part of the defences of Exeter Castle, which was built by William the Conqueror around 1068 after Exeter's rebellion against him. The gardens were created in the late 18th century, an oasis in the heart of the city.

Down at the lively quayside, the Custom House Visitor Centre tells the story of the city's maritime past. Exeter has had a quay since Roman times and the custom house was built in 1680 at the height of

Exeter's woollen-cloth industry boom. The building itself is worth a look, with its beautiful sweeping staircase.

The more adventurous can explore the waterways up close, on a kayak or canoe trail linking the Ship Canal with the River Exe, between the quayside and the Exe Estuary. The full circuit is 17km and takes about a day to complete. Several companies offer canoe and kayak hire on the quays.

Powderham Castle is located just outside the city, the ancestral seat of the Earls of Devon and still home to the current earl and countess and their children. The Manor of Powderham was first mentioned in the *Domesday Book* and has since come through battles and sieges, restorations and revivals. It has been open to visitors since 1959, set in wonderful parkland surroundings and gardens, with resident deer.

Staying with the stately home theme, Killerton is a Georgian mansion set in over 6,000 acres of beautiful Devon countryside. Dating from the 18th century and owned by the National Trust, outdoor enthusiasts will love the large choice of guided themed walks around the grounds, offering everything from butterfly walks to ancient tree discoveries. The house itself has an excellent collection of paintings, ceramics, period furniture and costumes from days gone by.

While you're in Devon, don't miss the Jurassic Coast, the World Heritage Site comprising 95 miles of coastline. The layers of sedimentary rock along the coast reveal the history of planet earth across 185 million years and form a record of the Triassic, Jurassic and Cretaceous periods. It stretches from Exmouth in East Devon to Studland Bay in Dorset.

For an atmospheric place to stay, check into the Exeter Hotel du Vin, a former 19th-century eye hospital spruced up into über-chic boutique hotel. Its attractive red-brick exterior with high Victorian sash windows gives way to chilled-out spaces inside. There's a great blend of old and new throughout the building with original Victorian tiles in the hallway and blazing log fires in the library.

Exeter is very well serviced by train and bus connections, and its two train stations offer regular links to London and the south-west.

Chapter 6

St Davids

From Wales, across the world, the wandering patron saint who founded a cathedral city

St Davids Cathedral. (© *Bernadette Fallon*)

Walking down the gentle slope from the city of St Davids, the cathedral unfolds itself dramatically against the sky, stretched across a lush green valley and enjoying one of the most stunning settings of any cathedral in the country. It is built on the site of St Davids Monastery, the former priory that became a place of pilgrimage after David's death in 589, eight years before St Augustine arrived in Kent to spread Christianity.

This site was a centre of Christian worship and pilgrimage long before the pope sent Augustine to convert the Saxons. David, who is the patron saint of Wales and known as *Dewi Sant* in Welsh, was born here and founded several monastic communities before establishing the largest here in the area that now bears his name.

There are many legends told of him and many miracles associated with his name, starting from birth when a blind man was reportedly cured by touching his baptismal water. He is said to be the son of Sant, a prince of Ceredigion, and Non, a noblewoman who became St Non. It is also said he was the nephew of King Arthur. Though that fact is much disputed. As is the existence of King Arthur.

But the story told is this: David grew up to become a priest and a missionary, not only travelling across Wales and England to spread Christianity, but also into Europe and as far as Jerusalem, where it's likely he was first anointed a bishop. He attended the Synod of Brefi in 550, when one of his chief miracles occurred. Unable to be heard in the crowd, a dove landed on his shoulder, blessing him with the Holy Spirit, and David rose magically from the ground to speak. He was then named Archbishop of Wales and, after all of his travelling, devoted himself to his Welsh monastery where he lived to the end of his life.

Buried in a shrine in the priory he founded, pilgrims flocked to venerate him and the monastery grew in importance as a place of spiritual and intellectual learning. When King Alfred the Great needed help rebuilding the intellectual life of Wessex in the 9th century, he called on Asser, a monk of St Davids, to help him. Asser later wrote *The Life of King Alfred*, which is the main source of information for the legendary king's life.

Even after the shrine was plundered and destroyed by Vikings in the 10th century, the pilgrims continued to come. William the Conqueror himself visited as a pilgrim in 1081. The fame of the cathedral grew even more after the first Norman bishop, Bernard, persuaded Pope Callixtus II to canonise David a saint at the start of the 12th century. And not only that, but to issue the following decree: that two pilgrimages made to St Davids were the equivalent of a pilgrimage to Rome – and three equalled a trip to Jerusalem. That sewed it up for St Davids. The cathedral was now firmly on the pilgrim map and the wealth flowed in. You can still see it today in the treasury. The magnificent artefacts that were uncovered in the bishops' graves, found beneath the floor of the nave, date back to those early times.

Work on a new cathedral began to host the increased numbers of visitors. When King Henry II visited towards the end of the 12th century – we'll find out more about the possible reasons why later on – its fame grew again. They were going to need a bigger building.

The nave of that building is the one you see today, started in 1181, and the oldest part of the cathedral. It is of a basic Romanesque design with its rounded, mighty pillars. Though there is one exception. Look up at the arches. Each one is carved with a completely different decoration, all reminiscent of Celtic strapwork design, making this a uniquely Celtic and local feature in a building style that originated in Norman France.

The arches are mighty, but they're not straight. Towards the top of the nave the arches lean out slightly, which may be due to the cathedral's situation on the side of a valley. There are also reports of an earthquake in the 13th century, which could have caused movement in the building. Towards the rood screen, the arches become more pointed, demonstrating the architectural styles straddled by the building – Romanesque and Gothic – making this a Transitional Romanesque building.

The magnificent Tudor timber ceiling in the nave dates from the 1530s and it has a whole book devoted to it in the cathedral gift shop. Built from oak, it features ornate carvings such as the Pagan green man and the Renaissance-influenced dragon-shaped dolphins. The ceilings throughout the cathedral are one of its most striking features, such as the beautifully coloured 15th-century Presbytery roof and wonderful fan vaulting in the Holy Trinity Chapel.

St Davids nave. (© *Bernadette Fallon*)

You can see from the pillars that abruptly stop part-way up the wall how much lower the nave aisles used to be. Bishop Gower had them raised in the 14th century to install bigger windows and allow in more light. He also built the ornate stone screen separating the nave from the aisle. Which conveniently gave him a prime position for his own tomb, located on the right-hand side.

The west wall was rebuilt a few times in fact. The original had large circular windows, quite low down in the wall. John Nash made the structure more elaborate when he worked on the cathedral in the late 1700s and moved the windows up. Working on a further restoration from 1862 to 1877, Sir Gilbert Scott didn't like this and moved them back down again. Interestingly, you can still see the outlines of each of the window placings, making it an unusual feature at the back of the cathedral. And, speaking of outlines, look for the traces of the 'ghostly knight' on one of the nave pillars, the last remnants of a medieval wall-painting that speaks to us from centuries ago.

Don't miss: centuries of change in the presbytery

Many centuries of building and restoration have gone into creating today's cathedral, and the beautiful presbytery is one of the most interesting places to see evidence of this. The pillars reveal a complex architectural history – some are round, some are octagonal and none of them matches the arcade. The walls are now higher than they originally were, the roof dates from the 15th century, part of the floor from the 16th century, and the rest from Victorian times.

The gold mosaics in the arches behind the great altar are 19th-century, placed in a triple lancet window that dates from 1221. And while the roof dates back to the 15th century, its paintwork was recoloured during Gilbert Scott's Victorian restoration. A large floor mirror allows you to admire it in all of its splendour.

Curious facts: the queen in the quire

In the quire next door, the cathedra, or bishop's throne, was probably constructed during the time of Bishop Gower in the 14th century, while the choir stalls date from the late 15th and early 16th centuries. There are some wonderful misericords here, carved under the canons' seats. Look out for the collection of pigs attacking a wolf, the

Presbytery ceiling. (© *Bernadette Fallon*)

bishop with the body of a goose chatting to a woman with the head of a goose, and the rather unusual man vomiting from a boat.

There are also sixty little heads carved around the walls over the seats of the stalls. Unusually, one of those seats belongs to the queen.

Misericord carving. (© *Bernadette Fallon*)

The reason why the reigning sovereign was granted a seat among the choristers is not known, but so far Queen Elizabeth II has sat in it four times, between 1955 and 2001. Her visit in 1995 resulted in St Davids regaining its city status. It is now the smallest city in Great Britain.

If you stand facing the nave, you will see a fragment of medieval painting that escaped the destruction of the 16th and 17th centuries, over the arched doorway of the screen. And it's lucky this part of the building – or, in fact, any of it – survived at all. After the Civil War, the presbytery arches were blocked up and aisles were roofless, open to the weather. The damage to the 16th-century floor tiles in the presbytery, however, was mainly caused by hoofs, as the troops rode their horses over them.

Don't miss: the new shrine of St David

The damage all started with the Reformation, when Henry VIII split with the Church of Rome to establish the Church of England and Wales, and banished all religious idols as a sign of popery. The shrine of St David, dating from 1275 and the source of much of the church's fame and wealth, was attacked and defaced. In 2010, an appeal to restore it was launched and on St David's Day – 1 March – in 2012, the new shrine was unveiled.

The old stonework has been updated with five new icons, painted by local artist Sarah Crisp. In the centre is St David with the unusual tonsure, common to monks in this area, where the head was not shaved at the top but at the front. The dove about to settle on his shoulder marks the miracle of Synod of Brefi, when David was raised up to speak to the crowd with a dove on his shoulder.

David is flanked by Patrick, the patron saint of Ireland, and Andrew, the patron saint of Scotland. But the fact they represent the three Celtic nations of the British Isles is a mere coincidence, as each have their own connection to this area. Patrick is said to have spent time as a missionary here in the 5th century before returning to Ireland, where he had once been a slave, to preach Christianity. In some versions of Patrick's story, he's said to have been born in Wales, in others England. Some legends have him predicting David's birth during his time in this area.

While St Andrew never actually visited Wales, the full name of the cathedral is St Davids Cathedral of St David and St Andrew, marking the connection between the two missionaries who worked to spread the word of God. And Andrew was a fisherman. Another link with this coastal area of Pembrokeshire.

The shrine of St David. (© *Bernadette Fallon*)

Under the icons are the stone niches where the pilgrims used to kneel and the holes where they would put their hands to touch the saints' bones. Today there are two reliquaries in the niches, containing bones that were once thought to be the relics of St David and St Justinian – we'll come to St Justinian shortly. But the bones have been carbon-dated to the 10th century – and David and Justinian died in the 6th.

So, who was St Justinian? You'll find his icon on the back of the shrine, alongside that of St Non, David's mother. He was a monk who, legend says, was invited by David to become his confessor and abbot of the cathedral. But finding life in the remote monastic community even too much for his ascetic tastes, he took himself off to nearby Ramsey Island where he lived as a hermit. His body is said to be buried in St Davids and today the island is owned and run by the Royal Society for the Protection of Birds as a bird reserve.

St Non was David's mother, born in the 5th century and most likely a member of the local nobility. David's birthplace is said to be marked by the ruined chapel of St Non, a few miles outside the city of St Davids, close to the Pembrokeshire Coastal Path. A nearby well is said to have miraculously sprang up during a storm at the time of David's birth. It's now a holy well, said to have healing powers, and has been visited for centuries by pilgrims. The area is still a place of pilgrimage today, with a modern retreat centre located close to the ruined chapel.

Curious facts: the tomb of Edmund Tudor

Henry VIII's Reformation stripped the cathedral of the power of its saint, as David's shrine was defaced and its relics destroyed. The attack against the Catholic church and the pope was carried out through the dissolution of the monasteries between 1536 and 1541, as Henry sacked the institutions aligned most closely with the Roman church. But while the cathedral lost a saint in this period, it ironically gained a member of Henry's own royal family.

The tomb of Edmund Tudor sits close to the high altar, regal and impressive. Although he was never a king, Edmund gave his name to a royal dynasty. Half-brother to King Henry VI, he was the father of King Henry VII and grandfather to King Henry VIII. And it was Henry VIII's own actions that brought him to the cathedral after the dissolution of the monasteries rendered his body homeless.

The tomb of Edmund Tudor. (© *Bernadette Fallon*)

Edmund fought for Henry VI in the early stages of the Wars of the Roses but was imprisoned by the Yorkists at Carmarthen Castle. He died there of the plague in 1456 and was buried in nearby Greyfriars Priory. After the priory was sacked under Henry's orders, his body was taken to St Davids.

Don't miss: The Holy Trinity Chapel

Bishop Gower had the stone screen built in the nave to house his tomb but Bishop Vaughan went one better in the 16th century, building the chantry chapel known as the Holy Trinity Chapel for his. It stands out immediately for a very good reason, it's built from a completely different stone – oolitic limestone – to the rest of the cathedral.

Built in the Perpendicular style, the golden stones of the interior give it a very grand aspect, as does the wonderful fan vaulted ceiling. The modern altar here is a mix of masonry, made from fragments of early Christian monuments, medieval stonework and the original altar slab. Behind is the crucifixion cross, flanked on each side by James, Andrew, Paul and Peter – all identifiable by the objects they hold. James, the patron saint of pilgrims, with his pilgrim staff and satchel; Andrew with the diagonal cross on which he was crucified; Peter with the keys of the kingdom of heaven; and Paul, with the sword and book that show him to be both a martyr and a scholar. Above, the carved stonework is as delicate as lace.

The altar is flanked by statues. On one side, Bishop Vaughan himself and on the other, possibly one of the most frustrated men in the history of the cathedral, Giraldus Cambrensis, also called Gerald Of Wales, who lived from 1146 to 1223. He was an archdeacon and historian and his works provide a valuable record of life at the time. He travelled extensively throughout his life on both scholarly and military expeditions.

But his wish to be Bishop of St Davids was constantly thwarted. He was nominated but never appointed, perhaps because of his desire to make the see independent of Canterbury if he was. Which didn't find favour with either the Archbishop of Canterbury or the

Altar in the Holy Trinity Chapel. (© *Bernadette Fallon*)

King of England, who didn't want a rebel Welshman on their hands. He turned down several offers of bishoprics in both Ireland and Wales, holding out for St Davids, but the offer never came and he recorded his struggles with great frustration in his autobiography, *De rebus a se gestis.*

Take a look at the bottom of the wall opposite the altar before you leave the chapel. The stone protruding here may have formed part of the original cathedral, pre-dating the current building and forming part of its foundation.

The back of the cathedral, particularly the south chapel aisle and Lady Chapel, suffered the most damage in the time of Cromwell and, after lead was stripped from the roof here, it eventually fell in. A substantial benefactor, the Countess of Maidstone, paid for the restoration of the south aisle in 1907. She is buried here in a somewhat ostentatious manner, in a tomb of alabaster carved with Latin and Greek inscriptions.

The roof of the Lady Chapel was also remodelled and features eye-catching bosses, some of which are 16th-century survivors. The stained-glass east window from 1924 is by C.E. Kempe in his distinctive richly textured style. A Welsh service is said in this chapel every Sunday.

Curious facts: the link with Canterbury

We've already met Gerald of Wales and his ill-fated encounters with the Archbishop of Canterbury. But there's another connection with that important cathedral here in the Chapel of St Thomas Becket. It was created as a memorial to the ill-fated Archbishop of Canterbury, murdered in his own cathedral by four knights who were reportedly acting on the wishes of King Henry II. Maybe as part of his penance, Henry came to St Davids the year after Becket's murder, in 1171. Built in the early 13th century, this chapel was completely remodelled by Bishop Gower in the 14th century, and its ceiling dates from this period. It also has the Early English piscina from the original chapel.

Don't miss: treasure in the treasury

From the magnificent ornaments discovered in the graves of early bishops to embroidered altar frontals and clergy robes, the treasury promises what its name suggests. Described by the cathedral as 'treasures that are spiritual, intellectual and artistic', here you'll find gold rings, silver chalices and the gilded copper croziers carried by the bishops of St Davids 800 years ago.

The treasury was built following a millennium appeal for funds, and leads out into the newly restored cloisters, with its gallery, facility rooms and refectory. Here you'll find the Pembrokeshire Banner, the first of the Welsh county banners to be created. It was made to be carried in the national Saint David's Day Parade in Cardiff on St David's Day in 2009.

Through the arches, in the garden, you'll see the memorial statue that was donated by the Welsh Armenians in thanks for the long-standing support offered by the Church of Wales to the people of Armenia. Designed and sculpted by Mariam Torosyan, an Armenian artist based in Cardiff, it shows Mary holding the young Jesus, echoing an icon found on Armenian altars.

The beautiful sculpture is a reminder of the international links the cathedral still maintains, 1,500 years after its original founder David travelled the world to spread the faith.

Visiting St Davids Cathedral

There is no fixed admission fee to visit the cathedral, but visitors are asked to give a donation of £3 when visiting outside of service times.

St Davids: where to go and what to do

St Davids is the smallest city in Britain, and also one of its prettiest. In summer, it has the feel of a seaside town even though it's not actually on the coast – but the sea is only a short distance away.

Here you'll find shops selling toys for the beach, as well as surfing lessons and tickets for island boat trips, alongside plenty of al fresco cafés and bars. Several operators in the city offer boat trips, including whale-or dolphin-spotting cruises. You can also visit nearby Ramsey Island, the former island home of St Justinian and now a bird reserve, famous for its choughs – who are related to crows – and its grey seals.

Here too are independent shops full of bespoke local crafts and gifts, art galleries, a wonderful second-hand bookshop and little in the way of High Street brands other than a discreetly placed Fat Face and Crew Clothing Company. On the outskirts of the city, Oriel y Parc is a gallery featuring changing exhibitions from the Welsh National Museum and is also the place to pick up information on the nearby Pembrokeshire Coast National Park.

There are winding laneways and cobblestones, as well as tiny bridges over the River Alun. Streets slope gently down to the valley where the magnificent cathedral is spread out against the sky. Opposite, the ruined bishop's palace dates back to the time of the foundation of the cathedral and the courtyard is an atmospheric venue for open-air performances in summer.

Continue past the cathedral and the road rises once more to the Penrhiw Hotel, a boutique guesthouse in its own beautifully landscaped gardens, surrounded by a woodland walk. It has the feel of a stately home given a contemporary makeover, the comfort of old-style glamour with the modern convenience of in-room Nespresso machines and iPod docks. There are just six bedrooms in the main house, two in the guest residence in the garden, and nothing as crass as a reception desk to jar the feeling of being in a very stylish private home – just an inviting lounge and elegant study. Breakfast is served in the garden-view dining room, for dinner a complimentary transfer is provided to its sister hotel Twr y Felin, serving delicious local produce.

The hotel offers hire bicycles, a great way to explore the local area. For beaches, head for Whitesands Bay, a popular destination for surfers. There's a Neolithic burial chamber, dating back to around 4000BC, at the windswept and rocky St Davids Head nearby. Its huge capstone is almost 20 feet wide, supported by a side-stone over 3 feet tall. Or travel south to St Non's Bay, named after St David's mother and believed to be his birthplace. Here you can visit the 13th- century ruins of St Non's Chapel, as well as the holy well said to have miraculously sprung up at David's birth. Pre-dating this site's Christian significance, standing stones in a nearby field suggest the chapel was built close to an ancient Pagan stone circle. Today the area is still an important place of contemporary pilgrimage and a modern centre, St Non's, offers a variety of retreats and workshops, including spiritual, yoga and meditation programmes.

St Davids doesn't have a railway station, the nearest station is Haverfordwest, from where you can catch a bus and the journey takes approximately forty-five minutes. There are frequent train connections from Haverfordwest to Cardiff and other major Welsh cities.

Chapter 7

St Asaph's

The smallest cathedral in Great Britain

St Asaph's Cathedral. (© *Bernadette Fallon*)

In a tiny city, the second-smallest in Britain, you'll find the nation's smallest cathedral. St Asaph's measures just 182 feet from the west door to the east end and is 68 feet wide. And this city close to the north coast of Wales has an interesting connection with Scotland, which is the reason the cathedral exists here today.

In 560 St Kentigern, who is known elsewhere as St Mungo and is the founder and patron saint of the city of Glasgow, founded a religious community in this part of Wales. Mungo had an eventful past before his arrival. His mother was a Scottish princess who was raped and became pregnant, thrown from a cliff – survived – then banished in a boat to Fife where her son Mungo was born. It's said he was raised by Saint Serf and, as a young man, started his own ministry where Glasgow now stands.

But a strong anti-Christian movement in Strathclyde saw Mungo's own banishment and he came eventually to Wales. Initially joining the religious community of St David – who we've just met in the previous chapter – he then moved to the opposite side of the country, to what is now St Asaph's. Asaph, a local man, was Mungo's favourite pupil and, when Mungo was invited to return to Strathclyde, he appointed Asaph as successor to lead his monastery and church in 573.

The first recorded Bishop of St Asaph was Gilbert in 1143 and the first stone building on the site was erected by Bishop Hugh in 1239. Just over forty years later it was burned down by the soldiers of Edward I. Edward had built a castle at nearby Rhuddlan and, the story goes, wanted to move the cathedral to be close to his castle. One day the cathedral seemingly 'accidentally' caught fire when the king's soldiers were in the area and Edward offered a large sum of money for its rebuilding. Provided it was moved where he wanted it.

The bishop of the time, Bishop Anian, was despatched to Rome to ask the pope's permission to move the cathedral. He apparently took his time on the journey and the pope had died when he got there. Without a papal seal of approval, there could be no cathedral move. Edward was furious, but the people of St Asaph were delighted their cathedral had been saved and Anian became a local hero. He died in 1293 and his effigy still stands in the nave of the cathedral he is responsible for saving.

Not that it escaped without harm in later centuries. In 1402 Owain Glyndwr's troops set fire to the cathedral in protest at English rule.

St Asaph's nave from the quire. (© *Bernadette Fallon*)

Glyndwr was the last native Welsh man to hold the title of Prince of Wales and the building lost its roof in the battle. A local account from the time describes the damage done:

> *The Chirch Cathedral of Saint Asaph, with the steple, bells, quere, porch, and vestiary, with all other contentis, chaliz, vestiments, and other ornaments, as the bokes, stalls, deskes, altres, and all the aparaill longging to the same chirch, was brent and utterly destroyed, and in likewys the byshop's palays and all his other three mannoirs no styke left.*

A succession of bishops was responsible for raising the money to re-roof it from 1411 on, although it wasn't finally finished until the appointment of Bishop Redman in 1471. Roofless for a large part of the 15th century, you can still see the weather damage to the corbels in the nave.

Today we have a building that originally dates from 1285 with 15th-century additions, a tower that was built in 1391 and underpinned in 1932 to prevent it sinking, all given a 19th-century restoration in Victorian times.

Don't miss: the first Welsh bible

In the 16th century, one of the cathedral's great treasures was created, which still stands in a glass case in the nave. In 1588 the *Bible* was translated into Welsh for the first time by William Morgan, who became Bishop of St Asaph in 1601. The work, commissioned by Queen Elizabeth I, is credited with keeping the Welsh language alive for future generations.

William Morgan was the son of a tenant farmer from Ty Mawr in Wybrnant and worked on the translation during the time he was a parish priest in Llanrhaeadr ym Mochnant. To create balance and harmony, he intentionally used words from both the north and south of Wales in his translation. When the book was published, the bard Owain Gwynedd said, 'That which was dark for us, you have filled with light.'

It's ironic when you consider that the first translator of the Bible into English, William Tyndale, was executed for heresy in 1536. Even more ironic when just two years later, Henry VIII authorised the use of the Bible in English for the Church of England, a translation that was largely Tyndale's own work. Interestingly, the Welsh Bible was translated from the original Hebrew and Greek, rather than from English. Today the treasured bible is only used for ceremonial and historic services, such as the visit of Prince Charles in 2012, when St Asaph received its city status from Queen Elizabeth II.

Prince Charles played another important part in the building's history in 1968, when the roof of the nave was restored and decorated to celebrate his investiture as Prince of Wales. Fittingly it's made of Welsh oak. The arches underneath in the main body of the nave are simply made, without decoration or carving. Which led the great literary figure Dr Samuel Johnson to comment on their 'dignity and grandeur' when he visited. Look out for the intriguing masons' marks on the nave pillars.

Inside the front door, the font was rescued from the river where it had been used as a water trough for horses during the Civil War. The carving on one side has been restored but you can still see the original damage caused on the other. As in so many other cathedrals, the Civil War troops wreaked havoc on the building, though the windows in the nave, being of plain glass and without religious decoration, survived. Today the west window over the door features 20th-century stained-glass created as a memorial to Alfred George Edwards, the first Archbishop of Wales, appointed after the Church of England in Wales was disestablished in 1920. He had been appointed Bishop of St Asaph in 1889 and is buried here.

Don't miss: 'Dr Livingstone, I presume'

The man who spoke those immortal words, Henry Morton Stanley, was a local boy. Born John Rowlands, the illegitimate son of a laundry maid, he was partly raised in St Asaph Workhouse. He was apprenticed as a ship's cabin boy as a young teenager and made his way to the USA in 1859, where he met Henry Hope Stanley, whose name he adopted. He worked as a solider in the American Civil War, a seaman for the US Navy, and eventually a journalist, reporting from Ethiopia, the Spanish Civil War and the Middle East. His later travels led him to discover Dr Livingstone, who had been missing since his departure for Africa in 1866 to search for the source of the Nile. He found the explorer on Lake Tanganyika in 1871, though both men record different dates for the meeting, ranging from late October to early November. Stanley's memorial in the nave of St Asaph's records him as an 'Explorer of Africa'.

A nearby memorial may not inspire such a familiar reaction but the first line of Felicia Hemans' most famous poem might. The poet, who lived for a time in St Asaph, wrote the poem *Casabianca* with its opening line 'The boy stood on the burning deck', first published in 1826. She died in Dublin in 1835.

Curious facts: the bodies in the transept

Fifteen years ago, the floor in the south transept was dug up to be replaced. A few early graves in the area were preserved, their stone slabs set into the ground here, but what was uncovered in the excavation was a much older burial ground, with up to thirty graves in a corner of the transept. Lying the bodies with the oldest skeletons on top formed a chronological record of the burials here in reverse order.

You'll find a much more modern 'body' on the wall. *The Naked Christ* is an arresting work by local sculptor Michelle Coxon, which has attracted some controversy for its very raw presentation of the crucified saviour. The sculpture is created from local materials, picked up by the artist on walks in the area, including tree roots, sheep bones and barbed wire.

The Naked Christ sculpture. (© *Bernadette Fallon*)

Nearby, the Spanish Madonna is thought to date from the 16th century. It was saved from one of the Spanish Armada ships that went down off the coast of Anglesey in 1588 and came into the possession of a famous political family, the Gladstones. It was eventually donated to the cathedral. It is delicately carved from ivory, a small reminder of a great sea tragedy.

Under the crossing, look up to see the angels holding a fish and a ring, which you'll find out more about at a nearby window. This area has been recently renovated to let more light into the building, with the removal of a screen across the side arch. A glass-topped altar has been installed in the nave, to conduct services closer to the congregation and show the cathedral as a modern place of worship. Both the altar and glass communion rails are the work of Robert Ingham of Cwm.

Don't miss: the carvings in the quire

The area of the presbytery was much restored by the Victorian architect Sir Gilbert Scott between 1869 and 1875. The canon stalls in the quire are the only medieval canopied canon stalls in north Wales and date from 1482. Here's the famous green man, looking out through his leaves from a pillar, and you'll also find a face that is presumed to be the master carver, William Frankelyn, above one of the stalls. The stalls used to occupy the space under the tower and you can see from the wood that the pillars here are not the originals. The originals were, in fact, used to tie up the horses of the troops in the Civil War and had to be replaced.

There are some fine examples of misericord carvings here, including a pattern worked by a master carver, alongside one by his apprentice. But the most poignant carving is actually a piece of graffiti, the name of one of the choristers, etched into the choir stall. It's Felix Powell, who along with his brother George won a competition to write a marching song for the First World War.

Green man. (© *Bernadette Fallon*)

The song *Pack Up Your Troubles in Your Old Kit Bag* became famous the world over, featured in the Laurel and Hardy film *Pack Up Your Troubles* in 1932 and was the inspiration for the title of Wilfred Owen's war poem, *Smile, Smile, Smile*, published in 1918.

Misericord master and apprentice carving. (© *Bernadette Fallon*)

It made the brothers music hall legends but Felix later suffered a breakdown in the First World War trenches. He took his own life during the Second World War in 1942.

The east window here tells the story of the life of Christ in glorious stained-glass colour. And if you look closely at the bottom of it, you will see a tiny frog etched into the religious representation – added apparently at the request of the artist's daughter. The bishop's throne dates to the 19th century and was once in the centre of the quire. It was believed to cover the grave of William Morgan, who translated the first bible into Welsh.

Back in the nave on the north side you'll find the story that reveals the meaning of the fish and the ring. The window here tells two stories of St Kentigern and St Asaph, recorded in *The Life of St Kentigern*, written by a monk named Jocelyn around the end of the 12th century. We also have Jocelyn to thank for the legend – or blame for the misinformation – of the founding of the church and monastery in the 6th century, as no historical or written record survives before this period.

A woman accused of adultery by her husband because she wasn't wearing her wedding ring, came to St Kentigern in despair. She said she had lost the ring and he advised her to go to the river, catch a fish and cook it. When she bit into the fish, there was her ring. It's probably fair to say that there is no archaeological evidence for this story.

The other half of the window depicts Asaph, carrying coals to the river to warm St Kentigern, as apparently the saint used to kneel in the water for penance. Despite the heat of the scalding hot coals, Asaph was never burned. Many of the windows in the cathedral were made by Ward and Hughes, but this one was made by Whitefriars in London. Look for the tiny friar in the bottom of the glass that is their emblem.

Curious facts: the return of the iron chest

The chest near the main door invites visitors to leave a donation for the upkeep of the cathedral. It dates from 1738, was originally used to

Eighteenth–centry iron chest. (© *Bernadette Fallon*)

store the church silver and is the work of a noted ironsmith, Robert
Davies from Croes Foel, near Wrexham. During recent renovations,
the chest was replaced by a more modern version in keeping with the

desire to update the cathedral. After it had been broken into three times, the 18th–century original was put back in its place.

Visiting St Asaph's Cathedral

The cathedral is free to visit but donations – into the sturdy iron chest – are welcomed. Tours may be booked in advance. Visit the website at Stasaph.churchinwales.org.uk for more information.

St Asaph: where to go and what to do

Located on the banks of the River Elwy, between Denbigh and the coastal resort of Rhyl, St Asaph is a great base for exploring the surrounding Welsh countryside with its mountain and moorland walks, as well as coastal attractions.

There are several riverside walks, including the rather romantically named 'Poachers' Trail' with its views to Snowdonia. From here you can also see St Beuno's College, where the poet and priest Gerard Manley Hopkins studied theology and wrote some of his best-loved poems including *The Windhover*, which he claimed was the best thing he'd ever written.

If you prefer not to travel on foot, there are several riding centres in the area so you can take in the local scenery on horseback. For anglers, there's fishing on the rivers Clwyd and Elwy, as well as at the Crydy Gwynt lake.

If you're travelling by train, you will most likely arrive into Rhyl from where you can get a bus to St Asaph. Buses run regularly and there are frequent train connections from Rhyl to Cardiff and other major Welsh cities. From Rhyl it's also an easy journey along the coast to the UNESCO-listed Conwy Castle and the attractive Victorian beach resort of Llandudno with its majestic promenade. The castle dates back to the time of Edward I, built between the end of the 13th century and the start of the 14th century, there's a largely intact great hall to visit, as well as a disembodied head in the king's apartments.

If you're staying in St Asaph, the Oriel Country Hotel and Spa is set in pleasant grounds and is just a short walk from the cathedral. The conservatory lounge is a beautiful light-filled space for a meal or a drink, and if you're there in good weather, there's an outdoor terrace by the pretty garden where you can dine *al fresco*.

Glossary

Act of Supremacy
The English act of Parliament passed in 1534 to recognise King Henry VIII as the supreme head of the Church of England, replacing the pope. The act was repealed in 1555 under the rule of his eldest daughter, the Catholic Queen Mary, but adopted again during the reign of his second daughter, Queen Elizabeth I

Aisle
A passage running parallel to a cathedral's nave and usually separated from it by piers, columns and arches

Altar
A table of wood or stone behind which the priest and clergy stand during the order of service and upon which holy communion, also known as the eucharist, is celebrated

Anglican church
Part of the Church of England, the reformed church that was established by the English Reformation in the 16th century in opposition to the Roman Catholic church

Arcade
A series of arches supported by columns or piers, or a covered walkway enclosed by arches

Bishop
An important ordained member of the clergy and the head of a diocese, whose lineage descends from the twelve apostles of Jesus Christ, according to the Roman Catholic church, though not in the later Protestant religion

Bishopric
The see, office, diocese or district under a bishop's control

Boss
A richly detailed raised ceiling ornament, usually made from wood or stone

Buttress
An architectural structure built to support a wall

Canon
This term has several meanings in a church context, referring to an ordained member of a church, serving under a bishop; an ecclesiastical rule or law enacted by a council or church authority, as well as a collection of such ecclesiastical laws

Carrel
A small enclosure in a cloister, used for study and writing

Cathedra
The seat or throne of a bishop, from which the word cathedral comes

Catholic church
Part of the Roman Catholic church that was founded by Jesus Christ and is headed by the Bishop of Rome, known as the pope

Chancel
The part of the church near the altar, often enclosed, and at one time reserved solely for the clergy and church officials

Chantry chapels
Pre-Reformation chapels funded by wealthy individuals or families, where priests were employed to say daily masses for the souls of the departed family members. The majority of these were destroyed during the Reformation.

Chapel
A recess or small room within a church or cathedral building for quiet prayer and reflection, usually containing an altar and often dedicated to a saint

Chapter house
The building or room where the cathedral's chapter meets; in Anglican and Catholic canon law a chapter is a college (chapter) of clerics formed to advise a bishop

Choir
A group of singers who mainly perform in church services

Choir (also known as Quire)
The part of the chancel between the sanctuary and nave that is normally reserved for the choir and church clergy, and usually richly decorated

Choir stall
A seat in the choir that is often ornately styled and decorated

Church of England
The English branch of the western Christian church that was established during the 16th-century Reformation by Henry VIII,

rejecting the pope's authority and bringing the church under control of the monarch

Clerestory
The upper level of the nave, transepts and choir, containing windows

Cloister
A covered outdoor passageway, usually built against one wall of the building and open on the other side with pillars

Crossing
The part of the building where the nave and transepts meet

Cruciform
A ground plan that is laid out in the shape of a cross

Crypt
The vault underneath a church that is usually reserved for burial and tombs

Dean
The head of the chapter of a cathedral or collegiate church

Decorated Gothic
The second phase of Gothic architecture in the UK, following Early English, where simple shapes gave way to more complex curves, flying buttresses became popular forms of support and decorations on buildings became more detailed

Dedication
This is the act of consecrating an altar, church or other sacred building

Domesday Book
A survey of all land and property in the kingdom of William the Conqueror following his victory at the Battle of Hastings in 1066

Early English architecture
The early period of English Gothic architecture that flourished at the end of the 12th century for 100 years, featuring pointed arches and ribbed vaults and favouring simple lines and fine proportion instead of elaborate decoration

Effigy
A sculpture or model of a person, often created to adorn a tomb

Font
A large basin used for baptisms, often ornately decorated and usually supported on a column

Gothic style
A type of architecture popular from the 12th to the 16th centuries, characterised by pointed rather than rounded arches, rib vaulting and taller slimmer buildings built to create the illusion of soaring up to heaven

Grisaille window
A stained-glass window created from glass in shades of greys and black

Green man
This motif is found in many cathedrals around the UK and in cultures around the world. Usually represented as a face surrounded by leaves, its origins are thought to be Pagan, symbolising the spirit of nature and the cycle of growth every spring

Lady Chapel

A chapel in a church that is dedicated to the Virgin Mary. Lady Chapels became popular in the later 12th and early 13th centuries, a time that saw a rise in the cult of the Virgin. They fell out of favour following Henry VIII's Reformation when the Blessed Virgin was no longer seen as worthy of special attention and was associated with Catholic idolatry

Lierne vault

An ornamental rib used in Gothic architecture that spans between two other ribs rather than from the centre

Magna Carta

Written in the 13th century, 'The Great Charter' established that everyone is subject to the law of the country, even the king. It also guarantees individual rights, the rights to justice and to a fair trial. It was first drafted by the Archbishop of Canterbury to make peace between King John and a group of his disgruntled barons and was signed by the king on 15 June 1215

Master mason

The leader of a building project, usually encompassing the roles of both architect and chief builder

Medieval

This refers to the period of time, also known as the Middle Ages, between the 5th and 15th centuries

Michaelmas

The feasts of saints Michael, Gabriel, Uriel and Raphael, also known as the archangels, celebrated in some churches either at the end of September or the start of November

Middle Ages

The period of time, also known as the medieval period, between the 5th and 15th centuries

Minster

A minster was the Anglo-Saxon name for a missionary church attached to a monastery, served by a community of priests, who went out and about preaching and 'ministering' to their congregations. Though the word is associated with Latin *monasterium* or monastery, the priests didn't live together under an abbot as part of a community, as monks did. The term dates back to the royal foundation charters of the 7th century, but with the establishment of parish churches from the 11th century, minsters became less common

Misericords

Tip-up seats designed to let clergy rest while standing during prayers. A ledge under the seat offers support when the seat is turned up – the word is derived from the Latin word for pity, as the seats were designed with old and infirm clergy in particular in mind

Mitre

A type of headgear worn by bishops

Nave

The main body of the cathedral running from the main entrance, which is normally in the west, to the quire. The word comes from the Latin word 'navis', which also gives us the word navy

Norman architecture

A form of architecture introduced to the UK by William the Conqueror, characterised by round arches, heavy masonry and buildings that are more squat than tall. It is also known as Romanesque

Pagan
A person holding religious beliefs other than those of the main world religions

Perpendicular style
The final stage of Gothic architecture in the UK, following Early English and Decorated styles, characterised by an emphasis on vertical lines

Piscina
A stone basin near the altar in Catholic and pre-Reformation churches for washing vessels used in the mass

Prebendary
A canon of a cathedral or collegiate church whose income originally came from a prebend, which was a portion of the institution's income

Precentor
A person in charge of the organisation of liturgy and worship in a cathedral, who may also be a canon or prebendary

Protestant church
A member of the western Christian churches that were separated from the Roman Catholic church in the Reformation, including the Baptist, Presbyterian and Lutheran churches

Pulpit
A raised stand or platform where a member of the clergy preaches and delivers sermons

Quire (also known as Choir)
The part of the chancel between the sanctuary and nave that is normally reserved for the choir and church clergy, and usually richly decorated

Reformation

The Reformation was the 16th-century movement that challenged papal authority and questioned the Catholic church's authority to define Christian practice. It was largely brought about in England by King Henry VIII's desire to elevate himself to head of the church so that he could secure a divorce from his first wife, Catherine of Aragon, to marry Anne Boleyn, a divorce that the head of the Catholic church, Pope Clement VII, refused to grant him. In 1534, the English parliament passed the Act of Supremacy to recognise Henry as the supreme head of the Church of England. This gave Henry free reign to seize the assets of the English cathedrals and monasteries, a considerable fortune consisting of property and possessions that had been in the hands of the church since Anglo–Saxon times. As well as re-distributing wealth into the hands of the king, many important church possessions were destroyed to remove traces of 'popish' Catholic faith and embrace a new more austere religion

Relics

Body parts or belongings of a deceased holy person, kept as objects of reverence

Reredos

The ornamental screen or cloth behind an altar, designed to give the congregation a visual focus as they receive communion

Rood

A crucifix, specifically at the entrance to a chancel

Rood screen

A partition separating the end of the nave from the entrance to the chancel that supports the rood. Also known as a choir screen, chancel screen or jube

Sanctuary
The most sacred part of the church, containing the altar

Scissor arches
Also known as strainer arches, used to support heavy building weight

See
The seat, centre of authority, office, or jurisdiction of a bishop

Strapwork
Stylised representation of interwoven straps in elaborate designs and patterns

Tournai fonts
Iconic baptismal fonts carved from black limestone in the 12th and early 13th centuries in the area of Tournai in Belgium. There are seven of these fonts in England

Transept
The passageway either side of the nave, creating the 'arms' of the cross in the cruciform floor plan, usually running north to south with the nave running west to east

True cross
The actual cross upon which Jesus Christ was crucified

Triforium
A shallow arched gallery above the nave of a cathedral, usually located below the clerestory

Further Reading

A History of Wales, John Davies (Penguin, 2007)

A Memoir of Jane Austen, James Edward Austen-Leigh (Oxford World's Classics, 2008)

Ancient Cathedrals of Wales: Their Story and Music, Meurig Owen, (Llygad Gwalch Cyf, 2013)

Bring Up The Bodies, Hilary Mantel (Fourth Estate, 2012)

England's Cathedrals, Simon Jenkins (Little, Brown, 2016)

Exeter Cathedral: A Short History and Description, Audrey Erskine, Vyvyan Hope, John Lloyd (Exeter Cathedral, 1988)

Gloucester Cathedral, Susan Hamilton (Scala Publishers, 2011)

Salisbury Cathedral: The Making of a Medieval Masterpiece, Timothy Tatton-Brown (Scala Publishers, 2009)

St Davids Cathedral, J. Wyn Evans (Pitkin, 2001)

St Davids and Dewisland: A Social History, David W. James (University of Wales Press, 2013)

The Ecclesiastical History of the English People, The Venerable Bede (Courier Corporation, 2012)

The English Cathedral, Peter Marlow (Merrell, 2012)

The History of England Volume I: Foundation, Peter Ackroyd (Pan, 2012)

The History of England Volume II: Tudors, Peter Ackroyd (Pan, 2013)

The History of England Volume III: Civil War, Peter Ackroyd (Pan, 2015)

Tile and Timber, Stone and Glass: Craftsmen of Winchester Cathedral, John Crook (Pitkin, 1992)

Wells Cathedral: An Architectural & Historical Guide, Elsa van der Zee (Close Publications, 2012)

Wolf Hall, Hilary Mantel (Fourth Estate, 2010)

Index